SEEDS OF LIBERTY

1688 and the Shaping of Modern Britain

John Miller

SOUVENIR PRESS

First published 1988 by Souvenir Press Ltd,
43 Great Russell Street, London WC1B 3PA
and simultaneously in Canada

ISBN 0 285 62839 9

Printed in Great Britain by
BAS Printers Limited, Over Wallop, Hampshire

CONTENTS

LIST OF ILLUSTRATIONS

PREFACE

Throughout history most societies have stressed the importance of their past, of the accumulated wisdom and experience of earlier generations. When literacy is rare people learn orally from their elders their ideas and values, their knowledge of farming and remedies for disease. It is not only the illiterate, however, who have sought to learn from the past. Belief in the possibility of progress is a recent development, which in seventeenth-century England was professed by only an advanced few. England's system of law, with its emphasis on precedent, encouraged men to look to the past for guidance on right and wrong. Traditional Christian teaching rested on a low view of man's capacity for virtue or improvement: he was irremediably sinful, the world was a snare and a delusion, perfection could be found only in the after-life. Many seventeenth-century English people eagerly looked forward to the end of the world and the saints' everlasting rest. Such intellectual obstacles to a belief in progress were reinforced by the simple fact that, for most people, life never seemed to get any better. It remained a struggle against hunger, cold, tedium and disease—in Hobbes's famous phrase, 'nasty, brutish and short'.

It was within this mental framework that people saw the two revolutions of Stuart England—the civil wars of the mid-century and the Revolution of 1688. 'Revolution' to them did not mean what it means to us. Since the French and industrial revolutions we have come to see a 'revolution' as a radical break, in which an old order is destroyed, making way for something very different. Within a view of history as the study of development from one state of things to another, as a linear progression, 'revolutions' are seen as periods of dramatically accelerated development. Seventeenth-century England lacked this sense of substantial change over time. History was seen as cyclical: essentially similar situations repeated themselves so that, despite upheavals and fluctuations, in the long run things remained much as before. 'Revolution' thus implied a circular movement which, after various vicissitudes, led back to the point of departure.

It was in this sense that most contemporaries saw what happened in 1688–9 as a 'revolution'—as a return to normality after a threat of change. Like most pre-industrial societies, that of Stuart England was basically conservative: most assumed that the farming techniques, laws and government of their ancestors were the best that there could be. They saw the lessons of history as relevant to the present and argued heatedly about the significance of the Norman Conquest and of the deposition of Richard II, as matters not of antiquarian but of contemporary significance. Later generations, therefore, saw the Revolution of 1688 as having played a major part in creating the world in which they lived. But how was it to be interpreted? As we shall see, later perceptions of the Revolution differed considerably and often grossly misrepresented what had happened. Moreover, many consequences of the Revolution were by no means intended by those who made it. While trying to distinguish between myth and reality, intent and outcome, however, one should remember that myth can influence events as strongly as reality can. People may act upon misconceptions, but the consequences of their actions are no less real for that. Conversely, if things did not turn out as contemporaries hoped or intended, it does not mean that their hopes and intentions were either unrealistic or unimportant. History has usually been written by the victors—in the case of 1688, by the Whigs. That does not mean that the losers, the Tories and Jacobites, were foolish, wrong, bad, insignificant or doomed to fail. However reluctant some historians may be to admit it, history is neither predictable nor inexorable. Luck—the outcome of a battle, the whim of a prince, the death of an heir, a change in the virulence of a microbe—can play a crucial part.

This book attempts to assess the significance of the Revolution of 1688. It deals mostly, not with high politics, but with its impact on the ordinary citizen whose views are not easy to discover. Illiteracy remained high and only a small minority of the literate committed their views to paper in a form which has survived: to accumulate a family archive required space and a strong sense of family continuity. The views of the 'lower orders' have often come down to us at second hand: through the eyes of their social superiors or of foreign visitors, through formal documents and legal records. Our understanding of 'the people' in eighteenth-century Britain is thus bound to be imperfect, a fact which should be borne in mind in the pages that follow.

A Note on Dates
Throughout, dates given in the text are old style—according to the calendar used in Britain, which was ten (later eleven) days behind the more accurate calendar in use on the continent. The year, however, is given as starting on 1 January, not 25 March. The continued use of the old calendar helps explain why contemporaries talked of the Revolution of 1688, not 1688–9: the events of January to March 1688/9 were seen as having occurred in 1688.

CHAPTER ONE

INVASION

Around midday on Monday, 5 November 1688, a motley flotilla of some six hundred ships straggled into Torbay. The sun shone, the weather was unseasonably mild. While horses swam through the chilly water to the beach, small boats began to ferry ashore some fourteen thousand soldiers. Most were foreign—Dutch, French, Germans, Danes—but they were warmly welcomed by the local people. Their leader was small, about five feet five inches, with a hooked nose and a hacking cough. It was the day after his thirty-eighth birthday, but he had been a major European figure since 1672, when French armies had overrun his native country, the Dutch Republic. In the shock of defeat, the Dutch had lynched their leader, Jan de Witt, and turned to the head of the family which had so often served so well in the Republic's highest offices: William III, Prince of Orange.

William's invasion of England was, by any standards, an extraordinary enterprise. In the seventeenth century military and naval campaigns were normally confined to the summer. In the winter roads became quagmires, bogging down provision carts and artillery; soldiers housed in tents and shacks fell sick and died in their thousands. At sea, wise sailors avoided the spring and autumn gales, which could scatter wooden ships like confetti: indeed, when William's fleet first set sail it was driven back by a storm. It then sailed south-west down the Channel, against the prevailing wind, but the wind veered to the east, helping the invasion force on its way and preventing the English fleet from leaving the Thames estuary—a meteorological change ascribed by contemporaries to divine intervention. Moreover, quite apart from all the other risks involved in mounting such an expedition at that time, William had made his preparations while there was a real risk that the French might attack the Dutch Republic. Had that happened, the Dutch could have spared no soldiers, so it was most fortunate for William that Louis XIV's armies became embroiled in the siege of Philippsburg, more than a hundred miles from the Dutch frontier.

William's invasion was thus, from a contemporary viewpoint, so risky as to verge on the foolhardy: clearly only the most imperative needs could justify the taking of such chances. Equally extraordinary was the reaction of the people of Devon: the English were notorious for their

An idealised representation of what must have been a confused process,
as William's forces landed at Torbay. From a Dutch print.
The Mansell Collection

hostility to foreigners, yet here they welcomed a foreign army as liberators. What had brought about such strange events? What had led William to appear in arms against the English king, James II, who was both his uncle and his father-in-law? And what had driven so many English people to see this foreigner as their deliverer?

*   *   *

Less than four years before, on 6 February 1685, James had succeeded his brother, Charles II, amid widespread rejoicing, which testified to the strength of England's monarchy. Foreigners regarded that monarchy as feeble: had not the English rebelled against and executed Charles I? In fact, although England's monarchy was eccentric and old-fashioned when judged against those in Europe, it was far from negligible. While kings like Louis XIV paraded their 'absolute' power and independence of their subjects, England's monarchy maintained an older tradition of mutual dependence between ruler and ruled. Unlike Louis, the Stuarts possessed neither an extensive bureaucracy nor a large standing army with which to impose their will. Instead, they relied on the leading men of each county and borough to dispense justice and to administer and defend the realm. By continental standards it was a ludicrously amateurish system and it was fortunate that the 'Dad's army' militia never had to defend England's shores against hardened troops. But the English were used to it and, for the larger landowners and more prosperous burghers, unpaid local office brought prestige and power; the Crown, meanwhile, lacking powerful means of coercion, posed little threat to their interests. For these reasons the ruling elite, through the institution of Parliament, extended the Crown's powers in the sixteenth century: the king's powers were seen not as a danger to his people but as an asset, for the functions which he performed—defence, justice, law and order—were for their benefit.

The monarchy's strength, then, lay not in its limited coercive powers but in people's willingness to co-operate in making government work. That co-operation depended on the king's behaving in ways that his subjects regarded as just and reasonable. If he used his powers not to protect his people, but (in their eyes) to oppress them, they would be far less willing to help him to govern. The limits on his power, and his people's rights against him, were believed to be defined, and secured, by the law. Under English common law, men could not be deprived of liberty or property without either their own consent through Parliament (notably through grants of taxation) or by due process of law: the jury system, especially, was seen as defending individual rights. The first two Stuarts, James I and Charles I, showed that their view of the law differed markedly from that of their subjects. They twisted and stretched traditional powers of the Crown—notably the power to raise money or to imprison 'dangerous' individuals in time of emergency—to a point where they seemed to be taxing and imprisoning at will. Traditions of government by consent, exemplified in Parliament, seemed under threat: England appeared to be moving towards a continental-style absolute monarchy. 'We are the last monarchy in Christendom that yet retain our ancient rights and liberties,' cried one MP: but for how long?

In the contests under the early Stuarts about the extent of the royal prerogative, the Crown was the aggressor. Charles I also supported a movement within the Church of England towards greater stress on 'the beauty of holiness', which many saw as leading England from Protestantism to Catholicism. Faced with what they saw as threats to liberty, property and religion, the members of Charles I's Parliaments sought to define his powers more precisely. He made concessions, but with obvious reluctance: he clearly intended to reverse those concessions at the first opportunity, using force if necessary. The impossibility of trusting him either to rule responsibly or to stick to what he had promised led, in 1642, to civil war. It was the king who first had recourse to arms; Parliament claimed that it followed suit only in self-defence and many Parliamentarians were embarrassed at being forced into rebellion: how could they justify it? If Parliament claimed a right to resist the king, it opened the way for the lower orders to resist Parliament. Indeed Parliament could justify its conduct only by virtue of its representing the people: was it reasonable, then, to deny the people the right to seek to impose their will on those who acted in their name?

Most Parliamentarians, then, made war on the king with reluctance and trepidation. Their worst fears were soon realised. Committed to winning the war at all costs, the Parliamentarian leaders proved more 'tyrannical' than Charles had ever been, riding roughshod over individual liberty and property rights and exacting the highest taxes which England had ever seen. Meanwhile, Parliament's challenge to the Crown stimulated radical challenges to the established order in Church and State. Until 1640 few questioned the need for a single national Church to maintain religious uniformity and moral discipline. Now sects emerged which claimed that nobody had the right to tell others what they should believe or how they should worship: an argument which threatened the Church's role as a force for social cohesion. Meanwhile, the Levellers roundly condemned the inequalities of English society. Why, they asked, should a few landlords and businessmen assume a right to rule over the rest of society? To be just, government had to rest on the consent of all of the governed and MPs should be truly responsible to those they represented, through frequent elections on a wide franchise.

The radical sects and Levellers alarmed the ruling elite, but they comprised only a small minority of the population. They could not have achieved any of their aims without the rise to power of the New Model Army. In establishing this army Parliament created a Frankenstein's monster which eventually turned on its creator. Religious and political radicalism became strong in the army, which came to see itself as the only embodiment of virtue and truth in a world of sinners and backsliders. Its leaders were under no illusions about their unpopularity. Indeed, the very fact that they had so little civilian support convinced them that they must be right: had Christ not said that only a chosen few would be saved? The army became convinced that there was no future in negotiating with Charles: it saw him as morally responsible for the bloodshed of the war and became convinced that he could not be trusted to keep to any agreement. In December 1648 it purged Parliament of all who would not agree to break off negotiations with the king. The following month he was tried and executed.

The civil war and Charles's execution were not the logical culmination of changes long in gestation, but the unexpected (and, for most, unwanted) consequences of his wilful refusal to keep within the rules and govern as his people expected. The widespread horror at his death, even in the Dutch Republic, was compounded by the next eleven years of military rule. The regimes of the 1650s were honest, efficient and (given their revolutionary origins) surprisingly moderate. They allowed an unprecedented degree of religious toleration, built up the navy and enhanced England's standing abroad, but they were not popular; they were seen as misanthropic and meddlesome. Taxes remained very high and civilian hostility to soldiers remained unabated. The sects were disliked as an exhibitionist minority, especially the Quakers with their open contempt for conventional authority. However admirable many aspects of the governments of the 1650s may have seemed to later centuries, people at the time did not want them. 'I am as much for government by consent as any man,' remarked Oliver Cromwell sadly, 'but where shall we find that consent?'

If the civil war and republic were an unwanted aberration, the restoration of monarchy in 1660 marked a return to normal. After a decade of self-righteously disinterested and diligent rule, of rigid sabbath observance and the prohibition of Christmas, people could return to the more relaxed rule of the old gentry families, bending national requirements to local needs. For the ruling elite, ousted from their cosy positions of power by zealots and upstarts, the first priority was to re-establish their dominance over Church, State and local government. The restoration of gentry rule also required the restoration of effective monarchy. Only a strong king could prevent the radicals from making another bid for power.

Besides, when Parliament had been forced in the 1640s to take on executive responsibilities—raising money, organizing armies—few MPs had enjoyed it: they were not full-time politicians, nor were they paid, and they found administration time-consuming, confusing and boring. They were thus content to let Charles II resume the king's traditional responsibility for the day-to-day direction of government.

The men who made the Restoration settlement hoped to return to the good old days before the reign of Charles I, when king and gentry ruled the nation in the best interests of everyone. This system had worked well enough then: why not now? For it to work properly, however, it was vital that the king should not appear to threaten the gentry's interests— their pre-eminence in local government, their property, liberty and religion. The Church of England was restored on essentially traditional lines: the Commons brusquely refused to allow toleration, using the full weight of the law to make the sects conform to the established Church. In the 1670s, however, hatred of Protestant Dissent was superseded by the fear of Popery, partly because of Charles's links with Catholic France, but more because his brother James became a Catholic. As Charles, despite his seventeen bastards, had no legitimate children, James was his heir presumptive, raising the possibility of England's first Catholic monarch since 'Bloody Mary'.

Anti-Catholicism was a central theme of seventeenth-century British history and played a vital part in the Revolution of 1688. There was much in it that was hysterical or irrational, but it had firm roots in past history and present experience. Ostensibly it was not religious in inspiration— Protestants claimed that Catholicism was too absurd to be taken seriously as a religion—but political. In power, it was alleged, Catholics persecuted Protestants cruelly and relentlessly; out of power they plotted unscrupulously against Protestant monarchs. By the later seventeenth century Catholicism was also equated with absolutism (or 'arbitrary government'). Priests used their spiritual influence to bend Catholic kings to their will, while absolute rulers used the Church to keep the people ignorant and subservient; thus priestly and kingly power reinforced one another. Hence many feared that if James became king he would raise a huge army, overturn the laws, collect taxation without consent and impose his adopted religion with implacable cruelty.

Following a supposed Popish Plot to murder the king, in 1678, fears such as these led to a sustained attempt to exclude James from the succession. The Exclusionists (or Whigs) won three successive general elections and three exclusion bills passed the Commons. Without the approval of the king and Lords, however, these could not become law, so the Whigs sought to put pressure on them by mobilising support outside Parliament, through propaganda, petitions and demonstrations; they also called for toleration for Dissenters. For many, the Whigs' conduct raised unpleasant echoes of the civil wars, of the overthrow of Church and monarchy and of 'the world turned upside down'. These 'Tories' saw such dangers as a far greater threat to their interests than James's possible misrule, *if* he became king: if he died before Charles, the problem would not arise. Increasingly, the struggle over Exclusion was not between the Whigs and the king but between Whig and Tory.

The Tories' emergence created a conservative backlash which Charles was to exploit in 1681–5. Like the civil war, the Exclusion Crisis bitterly divided the ruling elite. The Tories were reviled as favourers of Popery (for defending James's rights), they were cheated in elections and howled down by the Whig majority in the Commons. Hurt and angry, they wanted revenge, for which they needed the king's help. Their leaders were mostly peers and country gentlemen, who respected the laws and were inclined to be suspicious of central government. On this occasion, however, in their eagerness to crush the Whigs they went against their normal instincts. Against the Whig claim that the succession must be changed to save England from 'Popery and arbitrary government', they argued that God determined the succession and so it was not in Parliament's power to alter it. Faced with the Whig argument that Charles should comply with the wishes of his people, as expressed by the Commons, the Tories declared that his power came from God alone: the people were obliged to obey the king, rather than the other way round. This did not mean that the Tories believed that the king could do as he pleased: they assumed both conscience and common sense would keep him within the law and make him govern in his people's best interests (of which he was a far better judge than the 'giddy multitude'). Thus, while they in no way advocated unlimited royal power, they saw their main priority as buttressing the king's authority against the Whig threat, not restricting it.

Normally most Tories believed that the rules of law should be respected and that Parliament should meet often, but the years after the Exclusion Crisis were not normal times. The Whigs, in their eyes, had shown no regard for decency or justice, so they were entitled to respond in any way they could. They applauded when Charles removed the more assertive Whigs from county offices and put Tories in their places. Charles also appointed Tory judges and Tory sheriffs; the latter chose Tory jurors, who eagerly convicted any Whig or Dissenter who came before them. Many towns, however, possessed charters granted by the Crown under which the magistrates were at least nominally elected. The king could not remove them, under the existing charters, so (with the full co-operation of local Tories) pretexts were found to confiscate or surrender the charters. New ones were issued, which installed Tories in power and empowered the king to remove 'disaffected' members from the corporation in future.

For the Tories, this served a dual purpose. It ensured that magisterial power would be in safe hands (so that the laws against Dissent would be enforced) and strengthened the Tories' electoral position. Four-fifths of MPs represented boroughs. Most were small or had a restricted franchise, so that the corporation either elected the MPs or had a major say in who was elected. If the Tories could control the boroughs they would control the Commons: but until they did they showed little eagerness for Parliament to meet. They had been badly beaten in the elections of 1679–81, thanks (in their eyes) to Whig chicanery and rabble-rousing. They felt no compunction about using similar methods against the Whigs, but until they could do so effectively they forgot their normal preference for frequent Parliaments.

Some features of the 'Tory reaction' of 1681–5 were to figure in the Bill of Rights of 1689. The Whigs made great play of the Tories' misuse of the law courts and venerated the memory of 'martyrs' like Lord Russell and Algernon Sydney (executed on dubious treason charges) and the Earl of Essex (who cut his throat in the Tower). They denounced packed juries and 'cruel and unusual punishments': when Titus Oates, the fabricator of the Popish Plot, was convicted of multiple perjuries, which had led to the deaths of many innocent Catholics, the judges (unable to impose the death penalty) sentenced him to a flogging which was expected to kill him: it did not. When the homes of Whigs and Dissenters were searched after an alleged assassination plot, it was alleged that it was an infringement of liberty to treat good Protestants like Papists (who by law were forbidden to keep arms). When Tory magnates prosecuted former MPs for defamation in Parliamentary speeches, it was denounced as a breach of privilege. Such claims were plausible in themselves, but were somewhat one-sided. London's popularly-elected Whig sheriffs selected Whig juries which automatically acquitted any Whig who came before them. The Whigs' enthusiasm for free speech in Parliament did not extend to Tories expelled by the Whig majority for questioning the existence of the Popish Plot. It suited the Whigs to depict the Tories as the running-dogs of absolutism, bent on extending royal powers. The Tories, however, saw themselves as driven to make use of the king's prerogatives by the threat which the Whigs posed to Church and Crown. Neither party showed overmuch scruple. As one contemporary remarked: 'Tis now come to a civil war, not with the sword but law, and if the king cannot make his judges speak for him he will be beaten out of the field.'

The Tories, then, supported James's claim to the succession partly on grounds of natural justice—he ought not to be deprived of his birthright without trial—and partly because they saw the Whigs as posing the greater threat to their interests. They assumed that James would appreciate that he needed their support and so respect those interests; it was to be the Tories' tragedy that James did not see things the same way. By 1688 many had come to accept that the Whigs' gloomy predictions about James had been right. They then found the stand and the measures which they had earlier taken on his behalf acutely embarrassing.

*   *   *

James II was very different from his brother. Rigid where Charles was supple, hard-working where Charles was indolent, James was temperamentally inclined to the sort of strenuous measures which Charles avoided, while lacking the political acumen to appreciate that such measures might be dangerous. Like Charles I, James saw life in terms of simple polar opposites—good and evil, loyalty and sedition. Blessed with the mentality of a middle-ranking army officer, he had shown unswerving loyalty to his brother and now expected others to obey him equally uncritically. Such attitudes were ill suited to a system of government based on consent, but James had little time for pussyfooting considerations of prudence: he would do what he thought was right. He did not believe that he could do as he wished: he accepted that he would have to answer to God for his rule and that he was morally obliged to keep within the law. Unfortunately, however, his view of the law differed from that of most of his subjects. He had little patience with lawyers' subtleties, especially when these seemed inconsistent with what he saw as natural justice: a law which (to him) seemed manifestly unjust did not deserve to be treated as a law at all.

This would not have mattered had he left things as they were at his accession. The tide of Tory loyalism ran strongly for much of 1685. Their electoral preparations paid off: a strongly Tory House of Commons helped James to suppress a rising led by Charles's illegitimate son, the Duke of Monmouth, and voted him a larger revenue than any king had enjoyed for centuries. James was not, however, content to remain quietly at his ease. He wished to remove the laws which prevented Catholics from worshipping or competing for converts and excluded them from public office and Parliament. He saw these laws as unjust, the product of mindless prejudice and self-interest, and believed that if they were repealed, England's tiny Catholic community would grow rapidly. In the Tories' eyes, however, these laws were intended, not to prevent free and fair competition between Catholic and Protestant—Catholics never played fair—but to prevent the Catholics from achieving positions of power, in which they could persecute Protestants. What James saw as prejudice, they saw as self-preservation. James was enraged by their attitude. It showed, he said, that their pretended loyalty was a sham. He became increasingly vindictive

21

towards the Tory gentry and Anglican clergy. When the latter refused to desist from 'controversial' (anti-Catholic) preaching, he set up an ecclesiastical commission to punish disobedient clerics. This suspended the Bishop of London and expelled the fellows of Magdalen College, Oxford, for refusing to elect a Catholic as president: they were replaced by Catholics.

As James became aware that no Tory Parliament would repeal the laws against Catholics, the idea dawned of appealing to that other persecuted minority, the Dissenters. Surely, he reasoned, if they were allowed to worship and hold offices freely, they could not decently begrudge a similar freedom to the much smaller Catholic minority. But the laws against Dissenters and Catholics would have to be repealed by a Parliament. To secure a Dissenting Parliament James would have to extend his authority in two controversial ways. First, to encourage and to enable Dissenters to serve him, he would have to dispense them from the penalties of the laws against them *before* those laws were repealed by Parliament. He secured a ruling from his judges that he could dispense individuals from the penalties of law, as he saw fit, and used this to suspend all the laws against nonconformist worship, pending their repeal by Parliament. Second, he used all the powers of the Crown, and more, to manipulate elections and the electorate: he set out, in short, to pack the House of Commons with those who would do his bidding.

To James's unsubtle mind, it probably seemed that he was doing nothing illegal or novel. His judges had said he possessed a dispensing power: 'I am obliged to think what my judges do is according to law.' (He neglected to mention that he had secured this ruling only by dismissing judges who thought otherwise.) Moreover, the judges had assumed that he would use this dispensing power as previous kings had done: sparingly, in individual cases, where to apply the law rigorously would be contrary to natural justice. James, however, assumed that if he could dispense with the law in the case of one person, logically he could dispense the whole country from its penalties. Similarly, he probably saw his interference in the counties and boroughs as analogous to that promoted by the Tories in 1681–5. There were differences, however. The Tories were far more numerous, and socially and politically more influential, than the Dissenters. Charles had supported one section of the divided ruling elite against the other. James went outside the elite altogether, using his own authority to compensate for the Dissenters' innate lack of political weight. Moreover, whereas Charles had carefully kept within the terms of the boroughs' charters, James cheerfully appointed Dissenters to borough offices, although he usually had no legal right to do so.

In assessing the significance of the Revolution of 1688, James's true intentions are probably less important than the way his subjects perceived them. His main aim was to promote his religion: his extension of the dispensing power and campaign to pack Parliament were means to an end, not ends in themselves. His Protestant subjects, however, could not believe that anyone could take Catholicism seriously enough to risk everything in order to promote it; they therefore assumed that his real aim was to strengthen the monarchy. Given the supposed links between Catholicism and absolutism, they inevitably placed the worst possible construction on the actions of their Catholic king, but one did not need to be paranoid to fear that James was overturning England's constitution. Despite his obsession with fair play and talk of even-handedness, he shamelessly bullied and dismissed the judges and stretched the letter of the law so that it lost all touch with its spirit; he also consistently favoured Catholics and Dissenters and showed a vindictive spite towards Anglicans. By stretching his dispensing power to a point where he was suspending batches of statutes, he made nonsense of the principle that laws could be made or unmade only with Parliament's consent: where would it end? Meanwhile, had he succeeded in securing the election of his chosen candidates, the Commons would no longer have been a representative body. As he appointed bishops and created peers, he could also mould the Lords to his liking. Parliament would then be a 'rubber-stamp', composed as the king wished and bound to do his bidding. This was, indeed, a more serious threat (because more insidious) to government by consent than Charles I's attempt to rule without Parliament in the 1630s.

James's policies as king alienated the Tories as much as the Whigs, perhaps more. The Tories believed in Parliament and the rule of law: James's policies alarmed and outraged them. His promotion of Catholicism and his hostility to the Church provoked all but the most blinkered Anglican clergy to criticism and even defiance. Many Whigs, while enjoying the Tories' discomfiture, shared their alarm. Some Whigs, however, were sufficiently impressed by James's conversion to toleration to give him active support: many of his election agents in 1687–8 had learned their trade in support of Exclusion. The Tories' disillusionment, by contrast, was complete. In 1688 James ordered the Anglican clergy to read from their pulpits the Declaration of Indulgence, in which he suspended the laws against Catholics and Dissenters. Few obeyed and seven bishops petitioned against the order. James responded with a mixture of petulance, rigidity and folly. He called the petition a 'standard of rebellion' and prosecuted the bishops for seditious libel, in a show trial designed to underline his authority. It failed. The jury, amid wild rejoicing, acquitted the bishops and happy crowds celebrated by burning effigies of the Pope.

With all the sagacity of a lemming James had, by the summer of 1688, alienated his people to a degree which would have seemed incredible in 1685. Yet government did not collapse. Despite insults to priests and

Whereas Dissenters had denounced the bishops, in the Exclusion Crisis, as 'favourers of Popery', the Seven Bishops' trial led to their being portrayed as champions of Protestantism. Satirical print of 1688 by S. Gribelin. BBC Hulton Picture Library

Papists, law and order were maintained. James had built up a standing army of around twenty thousand men (which some saw as further evidence of his malign intentions). Despite some friction between Catholics and Protestants, the army seemed loyal and there was no force within England which could seriously challenge it. For the widespread disaffection to have any effect, outside intervention was needed, in the shape of William's army.

James married twice. By his first wife he had two daughters, Mary and Anne, both raised as Protestants. Mary in 1677 married William, her first cousin, in what turned out a happy, but childless, marriage. James's second wife, Mary of Modena, underwent numerous pregnancies, but none of her children survived infancy. William and Mary, as heirs presumptive, were a natural focus for opposition to James's regime, especially as the Dutch Republic was a haven for political and religious refugees. From 1686, some of William's English contacts urged him to intervene to save the nation from 'Popery and slavery'. William, however, had no wish to be used. Many in the Dutch Republic suspected that he wished to make himself king. Moreover, the crowned heads of Europe would not easily condone his making war on a rightful king, to whom he was so closely related. If William were to do as his English contacts proposed, he would need to have overwhelmingly strong reasons and to be able to justify his conduct to Dutch and European public opinion.

During 1687 and 1688, two developments gradually reduced his reticence. First, he became convinced that James, by hook or by crook, would deprive Mary of her claim to the throne. Late in 1687 it was announced that Mary of Modena was pregnant. Rumours abounded of a Jesuit plot to pass a 'suppositious' baby off as the queen's. As luck would have it, she did give birth to a son, who survived the eccentricities of seventeenth-century paediatrics and grew to manhood, showing that he had inherited all his father's intellectual limitations. Even before his birth, William had decided to invade and to secure his wife's claim. He was not personally ambitious and knew he would have no son to inherit his titles, but he was desperate to bring England, and its navy, into his lifelong struggle against Louis XIV. This brings us to the second development. By 1688 William, and most informed Dutchmen, believed that Louis and James were plotting secretly to attack the Republic. The invasion was thus a pre-emptive strike, to take England out before this attack could take place. Moreover, if the invasion could be presented as directed against France, it would be much more acceptable to rulers who would otherwise disapprove strongly of William's making war on his father-in-law, notably those habitual foes of France, the Holy Roman Emperor and the King of Spain.

In 1688 James repeatedly got the worst of both worlds. He rejoiced in the birth of his son—his prayers had at last been answered—but it hardened William's resolve and the prospect of an ongoing Catholic dynasty made his subjects more willing to countenance drastic measures: they could no longer presume that James's policies would collapse under the weight of their own impracticality. James also saw Louis's friendship as his greatest strength, but it turned out to be his greatest weakness. When the crunch came, Louis did nothing to help—his armies were bogged down on the Rhine, his fleet was in the Mediterranean—and his blustering claims that he was James's friend gave credence to the unfounded belief that there was a secret Anglo-French alliance. James would have to face the invading army, and the hostility of his subjects, alone.

CHAPTER TWO

REVOLUTION

From Torbay William moved to Exeter and waited for English notables to join him. He had brought with him few English or Scots of political weight and was unsure how far his contacts would live up to their promises to appear on his behalf. The greatest magnate in the south-west was the Earl of Bath, whose control over the small boroughs of Devon and Corn-wall had ensured that those counties sent a solid phalanx of Tory MPs to the 1685 Parliament. Since then, James's election agents had sought to undo all that he had achieved: now, he complained, 'all the interest is in one scale, and nothing but bare authority in the other'. Bath had assured William of his support, but, when William landed, Bath sat tight in Plymouth and did nothing—until it was clear that William was going to win. The first major recruit was a Tory, Edward Seymour, a man of monstrous pride, constantly disappointed that nobody else shared his impossibly high estimation of his own abilities. Seymour also drafted the Association, a promise to 'stick firm to this cause and to one another until our religion, laws and liberties are so far secured to us in a free Parliament that we shall be no more in danger of falling under Popery and slavery.' Where Seymour led, others followed: if cautious men did not wish to be the first to come in, no one wanted to be last.

How far this apparent lack of enthusiasm worried William is uncertain. His attitude to English support was ambivalent. Before agreeing to invade he had demanded a formal invitation, albeit signed by only seven men. They assured him 'there are nineteen parts of twenty of the people throughout the kingdom who are desirous of a change' and that James's army was riddled with disaffection. William, however, was reluctant to place much reliance on this: conspirators tend to be wildly over-optimistic about the support they can command. He brought a substantial army, but it was smaller than James's, even before he began to raise new regi-ments late in 1688. It would therefore be risky for William to take on James's army without English support, preferably in the form of a diver-sionary revolt to make James divide his forces. This may explain why he landed in the south-west. Four of the 'Immortal Seven' who signed the invitation had lands in the north; three (Danby, Devonshire and

and will take care to bring some good
Ingeneers with you, and we have
desired Mr H. to consult you about
all such matters, to whom we have
communicated our thoughts, in
many perticulars to tedious, to have
been written, and about which
no certain resolutions can be
taken, till wee have heard again
from your Highnesse:

25. 24. 27. 29. 31. 35. 33.

Sh: Dev: Dandy Lumly Lords Russ Sidney

The invitation to William, signed by the 'Immortal Seven', enabled him to claim that he was invading England at the request of the English. SP8/1, pt2, ff224–7. Crown Copyright material in the Public Record Office is reproduced by permission of the Controller of Her Majesty's Stationery Office

Delamere) were active in the northern risings later in November. William clearly hoped to use their support, without being used by them. He squashed Danby's attempt to set himself up as a latter-day Warwick the Kingmaker and made it clear that his main requirement was cavalry (above all peers and gentlemen); he did not want disorganised rustics armed with scythes and pitchforks.

As it turned out the military impact of the northern risings was less significant than that of riots in London, which forced James to keep a number of regiments there to maintain order. Their psychological and propaganda significance was much greater: indeed, the struggle between James and William was less a confrontation between armies than a battle for men's minds. William could succeed only if the bulk of James's subjects did nothing to oppose the invaders. Those whose principles stressed loyalty to the Crown were the Tories, but the extent of their disillusion-ment had been shown by the Seven Bishops' petition. When James made a determined bid for their support, in late September, he was assured that they would behave like honest men 'though they have been somewhat severely used of late'. The bishops argued that the best way for the king to rally support was to 'set all things back upon the foot they were at his coming to the crown'. If James wished to regain their support, he would have to pay for it with substantial concessions.

It was not in James's nature to make concessions. Not only did he believe that his policies had been morally right, but he feared that any sign of weakness would embolden his critics to demand more. As a result he conceded little and with obvious bad grace. He refused to grant the Tories' central demand for a free Parliament, on the grounds that there could be no free elections with a foreign army in the country. The Tories, for their part, showed little zeal to take up his cause. Apart from doubts about his willingness to change his ways, they had no intention of abandoning the strong bargaining position which William's coming had given them. When James asked the bishops and Tory peers to disavow William's somewhat exaggerated claim to have been invited by 'a great many lords, both spiritual and temporal', they replied that the proper place to give their opinion was in Parliament. When James tried to mobilise the militia against the invaders, he issued commissions to Tory peers and gentlemen whom he had earlier dismissed. Predictably their response was cool. Most did not refuse to serve, but raised tedious legal quibbles which provided a pretext to do nothing. Behind this foot-dragging lay simple resentment ('Some would think one kick of the breech enough for a gentle-man') plus a shrewd calculation that William's coming could force James to agree to a settlement highly acceptable to the Tories.

Such hopes were far from naïve. William had prepared the ground for his coming with an astute and widely distributed declaration, designed to win a broad basis of support. It concentrated on the grievances of James's reign, on which Whig and Tory could agree; it said nothing of the Tory reaction or the Whig 'martyrs' of Charles's last years. Conventionally, it blamed not the king but 'evil counsellors' who 'have overturned the religion, laws and liberties of these kingdoms' in a bid to establish 'arbitrary government'. It mentioned grievances which particularly affected Anglicans—the ecclesiastical commission, the expulsion of the fellows of Magdalen, the order to read the Declaration of Indulgence in the churches—while stressing William's wish to 'establish a good agreement between the Church of England and all Protestant Dissenters'. It condemned the employment of Catholics and opening of Catholic chapels contrary to law, the misuse of the dispensing power and the campaign to pack Parliament. Worst of all, to gain more time and facilitate their evil designs, these wicked counsellors had given out that the queen had had a son, although there was ample evidence during and after 'the queen's pretended bigness' that 'the pretended Prince of Wales' was not her child. To conclude, William assured the English that his only design was to have 'a free and lawful Parliament assembled as soon as is possible'.

William had been reluctant to give this assurance. He had hopes of the crown and regarded Parliament as no friend to the royal prerogative. Eventually, however, he bowed to his advisers' argument that without this commitment he would not win English support. It appealed especially to the Tories. They had won a crushing electoral victory in 1685 and, now that James was restoring them to local offices, they could expect to do well again. The Whigs would take time to rebuild their shattered electoral interests, which led some to insist that elections should be delayed. In these circumstances, it is not surprising that most Tories did nothing to oppose William, while some were active on his behalf: Danby seized York and a number of army officers (notably Lord Churchill, later Duke of Marlborough) defected to William.

If William's declaration appealed to both Whigs and Tories, and if neither did anything to help James, this did not mean that they co-operated amicably: past animosities were too deep. In the risings in the north, Danby kept aloof from the Whigs Devonshire and Delamere: only one Tory gentleman of any note joined the latter. Devonshire's followers, meeting at Nottingham, demanded an investigation of the deaths of the Whig 'martyrs'. Everywhere the Whigs used the Association in an effort to embarrass the Tories. Although it had been drafted by a Tory, many regarded the promise to live and die with William as incompatible with their oath of allegiance to James. Those who refused it were accused of lack of commitment to William's cause. Thus Whigs and Tories each tried to exploit William's invasion for their own advantage. The Whigs had no truck with James. Banking on William's defeating James and imposing terms upon him, they concentrated on lobbying William and on trying to poison his mind against the Tories. The Tories urged James to make concessions so extensive that they would remove any reason for William to remain in England: above all, they hoped that a free Parliament would reverse James's policies and ensure that nothing like them could be attempted in the future.

As so often, the Tories' strategy was realistic, but it was undermined by James's unpredictable behaviour. They reasoned that William would find it difficult, with inferior forces, to defeat James and so would have to negotiate, on the basis of his declaration. James, an experienced soldier with a proven record of courage, could be expected to offer effective resistance; in fact, although most of his soldiers proved loyal, he lost his nerve. Until June 1688 everything had seemed to go well. A firm believer in divine providence, he saw his victories over the Exclusionists and Monmouth as evidence that God had preserved him in order to propagate true religion. The birth of his son, giving him far more time to complete his designs, confirmed this view, but then everything fell apart. Louis XIV left him in the lurch, the Tories (for all their talk of loyalty) refused to help him. Even the wind turned against him. After William landed, reports of disaffection came in from all sides, with riots in London and risings in the north. When he advanced to Salisbury to confront William's army his scouts defected, so he had no idea where the enemy forces were and fell prey to alarmist rumours. Some officers in whom he had more than usual cause to trust—his nephew, Lord Cornbury, and Churchill—went over to William. His daughter, Anne, fled from court to the rebels in the north. He found it hard to sleep and was plagued by debilitating nose-bleeds. His resolve collapsed and he agreed to negotiate with William.

This was exactly what most Tories wanted. James even agreed to call a Parliament—but he had no intention of coming to terms. If Parliament met, he believed, it would force him to make humiliating concessions, drastically restricting his powers and reinforcing discrimination against Catholics. Above all, it would investigate the birth of his son, in order to disinherit him. James therefore negotiated in order to buy time, to get his wife and son out of the country: he would then follow them. In that way, he could reserve his position and preserve his son's title and then, one day, he would return (as his brother had done in 1660) to claim his own.

On the night of 10 December James fled, after ordering his commander-in-chief, the Earl of Feversham, to cease hostilities. Feversham interpreted this as an order to disband the army, which he did, without taking care to disarm the soldiers first. Most officers, however, submitted to William, leaving him in effective control of most of the forces in England. When he heard of James's flight, the undemonstrative William allowed himself

A Dutch print of 1690, emphasising the furtiveness, even cowardliness, of James's flight on 10 December, 1688. BBC Hulton Picture Library

a smile. He had maintained a delicate balance, keeping up the pressure on James (he had refused to halt his march on London during the negotiations) while avoiding subjecting his father-in-law to actual force, which would upset his wife and alienate European public opinion. William would have settled for less than James's expulsion and removal from the throne—a declaration of war against France and the disinheriting of the Prince of Wales would probably have sufficed—but he would prefer to become king. Thus James's flight was very satisfactory: William could secure his objective without using undue force. William was therefore most displeased to hear that James had been stopped in Kent by a group of fishermen and that he was on his way back to London.

Many Whigs saw James's flight as a renunciation of the crown, but for the Tories it was an embarrassment. James had gone out of his way to leave things in confusion, making no provision for the maintenance of order or the disbanding of his army and carrying off the Great Seal. On the other hand, many Tories now saw William as biased towards the

Whigs and Dissenters and had no wish to see him become king. Having taken a stand on non-resistance and the hereditary succession, they felt that they had been misled by William's declaration into going along with an act of resistance which seemed likely to lead to the removal of the lawful king. Driven by a mixture of pique, personal ambition and principled outrage, they resolved to maintain James's title and to stiffen his flagging resolution. It was hopeless. He no longer had an army and feared that, were he to stay, he would suffer his father's fate. William maintained his psychological pressure on the stricken king. No sooner had he returned to Whitehall than Dutch soldiers replaced the English guards and three emissaries came from William, in the middle of the night, to advise James to leave London 'for his own safety'. Next day, 18 December, he left London for Rochester with a Dutch escort. On the 23rd he fled again, to France.

Looking back at the events of 1688, the Tories focused not on the voluntary (and irresponsible) flight on 10 December but on James's expulsion from London on the 18th. In this way, they could argue that William had intended, from the start, to drive James out by force, a view which gained strength as the Tories became more disillusioned with William and with the Revolution. It had the merit (from their point of view) of exonerating James from blame for his departure and of allowing them to forget their own attempts to press James to come to terms with William. The fact remains, however, that it was James's psychological collapse and refusal to compromise that led to his leaving England and losing his throne. William would have settled for less, but James was not prepared to settle at all and so, yet again, cut the ground from under the Tories' feet. Their stress on non-resistance, on the hereditary succession and on the mutual dependence of Church and Crown was very much in tune with the beliefs and emotions of a conservative and religious age. It was logical that the hierarchies of Church, State and society should reinforce one another. James, however, threw over his natural supporters in the interests of a small and unpopular minority, the Catholics. He ignored the Tories' realistic advice to negotiate the best terms he could with William and gave them no support or direction as they struggled to preserve his right to the crown. Only an increasing dislike of William led the Tories to go on trying to serve a king who seemed so blind to his own best interests.

The Whigs gleefully exploited the Tories' discomfiture. Having backed the right horse (William) they claimed a monopoly of the credit for his success. They alleged that the Tories who appeared for William had jeopardised his cause by their slowness and half-heartedness. They used the Association to try to demonstrate the Tories' alleged lack of commitment. They harped on the misuse of law and power during the Tory reaction, about which William's declaration had said nothing. The Tories urged

33

William to stick to the terms of his declaration and threw every obstacle they could in the way of his becoming king. Late in December meetings of peers and former MPs asked him to summon a Convention (only a king could call a Parliament) for 22 January 1689. The elections produced a Whig majority in the Commons (the Association was widely used) but the Lords had a Tory majority, so that the settlement which emerged was something of a lowest common denominator. Besides, a quick settlement was vital. Parts of the army were mutinous, Ireland was being overrun by James's supporters. Only William could maintain order and secure Ireland: if, as he threatened, he returned to Holland, there would be chaos. William, however, did not wish to make the strength of his position too obvious, so as not to upset English and continental public opinion. He relied on informal pressures to achieve his ends, eliciting invitations to invade, to come to London, to assume control of the government, to call the Convention—and to become king.

The Convention's decision to offer the crown jointly to William and Mary was difficult to justify in theory, but was pragmatic and practical. Some Whigs felt that James should be deposed for misgovernment, but the Tory majority in the Lords would never have agreed and many Whigs had qualms about such a move. It was therefore argued that he had abdicated, leaving the throne vacant, so that it was up to the Convention to decide who should succeed him. Some Tories protested that this would make the monarchy elective, but their underlying concern was to prevent William's being made king. To that end, they argued, first, that William and Mary should act as regents for James, then that (with James's departure) the crown had already passed to Mary. William, however, was adamant that 'he could not resolve to accept of a dignity, so as to hold it only for the life of another': if Mary died before him, and he were only her consort, his authority would cease. Faced with his determination, the Tory peers' resolve crumbled. The Lords concurred with the Commons that the crown should be offered to William and Mary, but Tory consciences were eased in two ways. First, while William (third in line) overtook Anne (who was second), the transmission of the right to succeed was to follow strict hereditary order: first Mary's children, then Anne's, then any children William might have by a later marriage. Second, the oath of allegiance was modified, so that Tories would not have to call William a 'rightful and lawful' king.

While the Lords debated the succession, the Commons were drawing up a list of 'heads of grievances'. As the drafting committee was dominated by Whigs, the 'grievances' included some from the early 1680s (essentially Whig complaints against the Tories) as well as others from James's reign, upon which Whigs and Tories agreed. Both types appeared in the Declaration of Rights, which was read to William and Mary at the time of the offer of the crown and later passed into law as the Bill of Rights. This bequeathed to later generations the impression that royal policy in the 1680s had formed a single coherent design to establish 'arbitrary power', which the Tories had supported. This was typical of the way in which the Whigs tried to arrogate to themselves a monopoly of credit for the Revolution. The Tories offered little opposition to the Declaration of Rights for three reasons. First, their primary concern was the succession: some Tories supported the proposal to draw up grievances in the hope of annoying William and delaying a settlement. The Tory peers did not oppose several resolutions which went against their principles but did not relate directly to the succession: that James had broken the 'original contract' between king and people (whatever that meant) and that experience showed that to have a Popish king was incompatible with the safety of a Protestant kingdom. Second, underhand pressure from William and the need for a quick settlement led to the dropping of the more novel 'heads', which would require fresh legislation. What remained was largely conventional and so acceptable to the Tories. Third, to assume that the Tories would oppose restrictions on the king's prerogatives would be to accept the Whig claim that the Tories supported unfettered royal power: they did not. They had gone along with the misuse of the law in 1681–5 because they believed that they were engaged in a struggle to the death in which no holds were barred. Normally they resented the abuse of kingly power. Moreover, their dislike of William and fear of Whig reprisals gave them good reason to guard against the future misuse of executive power and of the legal system, for they would be the ones most likely to suffer.

The Declaration of Rights contained four main elements. First, the new watered-down oath of allegiance, designed to make it easier for Tories to serve the new regime. Second, the resolution against having a Catholic king: this was extended, in the Bill of Rights, into a provision excluding Catholics from the throne. Third, it regulated the succession. Finally, it recounted some of the 'grievances' of the last decade and informed the new rulers of the true state of the law on these points. It denounced the dispensing and suspending powers, the ecclesiastical commission, 'cruel and unusual punishments' and misuse of the jury system. It asserted various 'rights'—of subjects to petition, of MPs to free speech within Parliament, of Protestants to keep arms for their own defence. It stated that elections to Parliament should be 'free' and that Parliaments should be held 'frequently'. These assertions were conventional and had become the subject of contention only because kings had stretched their powers in recent years. Some dealt with 'grey areas', where the king had considerable discretion but, until the 1680s, had rarely used it controversially. The one new claim was that to have a standing army in peacetime, without Parliament's consent, was 'against law'. The army's legal status, and the

Crown's right to punish mutiny and desertion, had long been uncertain. The English saw standing armies as inimical to liberty, but, in practice, while the army had remained small, protests against it had been sporadic. When James enlarged it to more than twenty thousand men, however, anxiety increased and the Convention decreed that this should not happen again. It also passed a Mutiny Act, for the punishment of mutiny and desertion, but only for a limited period: if the Act was not renewed, the power would lapse.

William believed, correctly, that the Declaration of Rights did not seriously abridge his powers. He could still call and dismiss Parliaments, formulate policy and appoint officials. Yet he and his successors found it increasingly difficult to use those powers as they chose. This owed little to the Declaration's vague generalities: who could define what constituted a 'free' election? Given William's powerful position, he could not be forced to agree to legislation which would restrict his power: he always had the option of going home and leaving the English to their fate. But there was another way of limiting him, which he could not prevent as it did not require new legislation. In the debates on the 'grievances', some MPs put their finger on the real key to the settlement: 'All the revenue is in your hands, which fell with the last king and you may keep that back. Can he whom you place on the throne support the government without the revenue? Can he do good or harm without it?'

The reasoning was persuasive. The Commons failed to grant William all the revenues which Charles and James had enjoyed. Moreover, England soon embarked on a war with France which required vast amounts of money. To provide it, Parliament, formerly an occasional institution, met regularly, for several months each year. Sometimes, the Commons attached specific conditions to their grants, to which William (rather than lose his money) had to agree. More often, they did not need to. William learned to avoid actions which were legally within his powers but which would prove politically counter-productive. For instance, there was nothing in law to stop him dismissing judges at will, but he found it wiser not to do so. The Revolution thus marked the beginning of one major feature of the modern British constitution: the divergence between the monarch's still very extensive theoretical powers and the stringent limitations on the way in which those powers are used in practice.

The Revolution, then, brought about two major constitutional changes. First, Catholics were excluded from the throne: after James II, even Tories accepted that this was necessary. Second, the monarch's financial dependence on Parliament ensured that his powers were less extensive in practice than in theory. After 1688, the royal prerogative no longer threatened the liberty and property of the subject. This was achieved in an indirect, pragmatic manner. It was the product not of any ideological objection to kingly power, but of sad experience, which showed that the Stuarts could not be trusted to use the Crown's traditional powers responsibly: on this, Whig and Tory agreed. Both these changes were essentially negative, designed to prevent the recurrence of earlier abuses of royal power. They were seen as putting the mixed and balanced constitution back on to an even keel after attempts by Puritan radicals and would-be absolutist kings to overturn it. Many in later generations also saw 1688 as a 'preserving revolution'. To George Chalmers, writing in the 1790s, 'none of the old foundations of our government were weakened and none of the landmarks of the law were removed'. In the mid-nineteenth century, Lord Macaulay's view was similar:

> Not a single flower of the crown was touched. Not a single new right was given to the people . . . Some controverted points had been decided according to the sense of the best jurists and there had been a slight deviation from the ordinary course of the succession. This was all; and this was enough.

By halting the movement towards absolutism, England was (Macaulay thought) able to avoid the revolutions which, on the continent, were the outcome of the inevitable popular challenge to autocratic rule.

Chalmers' and Macaulay's view was common among later Whigs, but it was not the only one. Soon after the Declaration of Rights John Locke published his *Second Treatise of Government*. This argued that no form of government was inherently better than any other. Government could be justified only by its serving the interests of the governed. If it failed to do so, if any ruler abused his trust, the people could rise up and overthrow it; they could then establish a new government, prescribing for it such tasks and limits as they saw fit.

It seemed, to some, that this was what had happened in 1688, but in fact Locke's model bore little resemblance to what people did and said at the time. Those who took up arms mostly denied that they were rebels and failed to invoke the right to resist a tyrant. The Convention declared that James had abdicated, not that he had been deposed, and most saw the Declaration of Rights as a restatement of the old constitution, not as a blueprint for a new one. Moreover, many Whigs believed Locke's arguments smacked of democracy (which they equated with anarchy: the 'giddy multitude' lacked the wisdom or responsibility needed to exercise power). Locke's blanket endorsement of a right of resistance alarmed them. While it might be acceptable for aristocrats to call out their tenants in order to save themselves from Popish tyranny, it was dangerous to allow the people to reject any government they disliked. They were not reassured by Locke's observation that the people were unlikely to stir except under the gravest provocation and that experience suggested that new

Although William dismissed the pomp of monarchy as 'whipped cream'—all air and little substance—he was depicted in traditionally reverential terms in the painting which adorns the ceiling of the Painted Hall in the naval hospital which he founded at Greenwich. Greater London Photograph Library

forms of government were rarely very different from the old. Once the Whigs had a firm hold on power, after 1714, they were still less willing to countenance a right of resistance, which could be invoked only against them. Locke's argument that no government was sacrosanct, and that the people could change it if it did not meet their needs, was taken up by radical reformers: what right, asked Tom Paine, had the Parliament of 1688 to bind later generations? By contrast, the Whig establishment argued that the Revolution settlement was perfect, whether it marked a vindication of the old constitution or a new start. No further change was needed.

In one area only did the establishment Whigs argue that the Revolution had brought important changes. Most Whigs accepted monarchy as a traditional and necessary institution, but denied that kings had any supernatural attributes. While Tories asserted the divine right of kings, Whigs argued that kings' powers were rooted in history and law; the limits which these imposed reflected an 'original contract' between primitive kings and their subjects. Whigs claimed that the diversion of the succession in 1689 struck a fatal blow to both the hereditary principle and the divine right of kings: on this occasion Parliament, not God, determined the succession. However, it was possible to see this as only 'a small and temporary deviation' from the regular order of succession: when James and William died, and Anne succeeded, it would flow back into its proper channel—and in 1689 it seemed that Anne would have children. They all died, however, leaving an awkward choice between a Catholic Stuart (James's son, the Old Pretender) and a Protestant with a much weaker claim (Sophia, Electress of Hanover). Most Tories put their Protestantism before their legitimism and opted for Hanover, albeit with visible distaste. Even after this large hiccup in the succession, however, the Crown continued to pass through the male line. The mystical aura of monarchy survived, despite the Georges' unprepossessing demeanour. Logically, perhaps, it should not have done, but belief in divine right and reverence for monarchy had always depended less on logic than on an emotion, which remained remarkably resilient. Early eighteenth-century Tories remained emotionally attracted to the Stuarts, when self-interest and common sense should have led them to make their peace with the Hanoverians. Moreover, if the Georges (unlike James II and Anne) did not claim that their royal touch could cure the king's evil (scrofula), the iconography of monarchy remained little changed: Thornhill's representations of William and George I were in many ways similar to Rubens' apotheosis of James I.

These first two chapters have told the story of the Revolution of 1688 in England, mainly from the point of view of high politics. They have sought to show what happened and how subsequent representations of what happened were often inaccurate, partly because of factional bias, partly because of misunderstanding. It is now time to consider the Revolution's impact on the English people and on the people of Scotland and Ireland. First, however, we must look at the social order of seventeenth- and eighteenth-century England, in order to establish who was affected by the Revolution, and in what ways.

CHAPTER THREE

THE SORTS AND CONDITIONS OF MEN

In 1696 the statistician Gregory King drew up a table of 'ranks, degrees, titles and qualifications'; he assessed the number of households in each category and the average income of each household. He divided them into those who were 'increasing the wealth of the kingdom' (landowners, merchants, officials, farmers and the like) and those who were decreasing its wealth, by consuming more than they produced: notably 'labouring people and out-servants' and 'cottagers and paupers' (together these made up about one half of the population). In 1709 Daniel Defoe produced a simpler scheme.

1. The great, who live profusely.
2. The rich, who live plentifully.
3. The middle sort, who live well.
4. The working trade, who labour hard, but feel no want.
5. The country people, farmers, etc., who fare indifferently.
6. The poor, that fare hard.
7. The miserable, that really pinch and suffer want.

Both approaches have their problems. King tended to equate status with wealth, distinguishing 'knights' from 'esquires' and 'freeholders' from 'farmers'. Defoe considered only gradations of comfort without relating them to status or occupation. Neither used the modern term 'class', which came into use much later in the eighteenth century. Both, however, implicitly recognised the social differences between rural and urban communities.

England in 1688 was predominantly agricultural. The majority of people worked on the land and lived in villages and hamlets. Many others were involved in processing agricultural products: food and drink, cloth, leather. While there were plenty of navigable rivers, overland transport was slow and expensive. Market towns and their hinterlands (a radius of five to ten miles) were self-sufficient in most products, to a point which would be inconceivable today. Travel was difficult, and although many moved

40

from their place of birth in search of work (or land to rent), few migrated outside their region of origin. This ensured that localities retained a greater individuality than they do today. The most basic division was that between two major farming patterns. The first, essentially arable, was found mainly in the south and east. Grain growing required intensive cultivation and a large labour force, so arable villages tended to be large and compact. Where there was a resident squire, the villagers' lives were likely to be closely controlled. With space at a premium, newcomers without jobs or money were discouraged or excluded. The second form of farming, basically pastoral, was found in upland and forest regions. As the ancient forests were cleared, small settlements sprang up, whose livelihoods depended on cattle- and sheep-rearing, dairying and woodland crafts. Pastoral farming was extensive and needed less labour than arable, so the population was sparse, especially in the hills, where flocks migrated between winter and summer pastures. Villages consisted of a number of scattered hamlets and farmsteads. There was rarely a resident landlord and, even if there was, the dispersal of the population made it difficult to supervise and control their lives. There was thus a chance for squatters and cottagers to settle and to carve out a living as best they could. Contemporaries regarded nucleated arable villages as orderly and deferential, while pastoral and woodland settlements were seen as insubordinate, full of masterless men.

By their very nature, pastoral communities were less stratified, more egalitarian than grain-growing villages. In the latter, there developed over the centuries the tripartite division which became characteristic of English farming. At the top was a small elite of substantial landowners, peers and gentlemen. Some showed an interest in farming (especially when this became fashionable in the eighteenth century), but this was a matter of choice, not economic necessity. The bulk of their income came from rents, paid by the second, much larger, category—working farmers. These were usually divided into yeomen and husbandmen. The former farmed on a large enough scale to make substantial profits and often diversified, buying parcels of land, dealing in agricultural produce or lending money at interest. The most successful would build substantial houses, buy silver for the table and fine dresses for their wives and daughters, and mingle socially with the gentry. For the husbandman, life was harder. Producing on a smaller scale, his profits in a good year were too small to offset his losses in a bad one. He could not afford to undertake improvements (such as drainage works) which would increase the yield of his land. As profits fell and taxes rose, many were overwhelmed by debt, gave up their tenancies and sank into the third category, landless labourers. Here, too, there were gradations of wealth. Skilled craftsmen fared better than unskilled, those with cottage gardens, or access to commons where they

Most manufacturing throughout the eighteenth century took place in the home, especially in the textile industry, where the labour of women was of prime importance. Drawn and engraved by William Hincks, 1785. Brian Rooney collection

could graze a cow or pig, were better off than those without. In the half-century after 1688 real wages rose, on average, but many struggled by on irregular work, badly-paid, and whatever the parish provided in poor relief. Moreover, as time went by, these labourers became more numerous and more dependent on wages. Common rights were eaten away as land-lords 'rationalised' their estates, leasing the land to a few, large-scale yeomen farmers.

This tripartite division of rural society has one major weakness: it embraces only those working on the land. Most villages contained some engaged in non-agricultural crafts and, sometimes, large numbers of industrial workers. Until the nineteenth century, the major unit of manufacturing was not the factory but the home. England's greatest export, woollen cloth, was woven on tens of thousands of domestic looms; much industry remained rooted in the countryside. The huge sprawling parish of Halifax became a major cloth-making centre; in the Tyneside parish of Whickham coal-miners outnumbered farm-workers even at the start of the seventeenth century. Moreover, just as yeomen dabbled in other forms of money-making, many labouring families were involved in both agriculture and industry. The demand for agricultural labour was highly seasonal, the cloth industry was affected by fluctuations in demand: it made sense for families to spread their risks and to maximise the family's earning potential. Wives span yarn while husbands laboured in the fields; children scared birds and gathered stones.

Just as industry permeated the countryside, so agriculture infiltrated the towns. Most had markets: many were market centres and little else. Some, like Nottingham, had meadows in the heart of the town; often the fields around the town belonged to its inhabitants. England in 1688 had few large towns. London, with half a million people, differed from the rest both in degree and in kind. No other could boast a population of as much as fifty thousand; most were very much smaller. But despite their small size, towns made a vital contribution to the economy and possessed a distinctive social order, more fluid than that of the countryside. Wealth counted for more than inherited rank, fortunes were made and lost far more rapidly in trade and the professions than in agriculture. Urban society can be divided into three rough categories. First, those who worked for themselves. These ranged from self-employed craftsmen and shopkeepers, struggling to keep their families, up to successful merchants who could afford to devote some of their time to public affairs. This category would also include the professions—lawyers, the clergy, doctors, schoolmasters—although their prosperity varied greatly. Second, there were those who worked for others on a fairly regular basis: wage labourers and apprentices (the latter an ambivalent group, who hoped one day to be masters themselves). The third category were those lucky to work at all: casual labourers, beggars, vagrants, paupers, the old and the sick, the orphaned and the crippled, the criminal and the insane. Often drawn to the town by hopes of work or charity, they eked out a precarious living, feared as a source of crime and disease, a volatile and unwanted burden on the purses of the well-to-do.

In considering what the Revolution meant to the English, one must assess which sections of the people were aware of national events and which participated in government and politics. Apart from rumour and word of mouth, whose impact is incalculable, there were two main media of communication, the pulpit and the press. Before the Revolution, the former should in theory have reached almost every English person. Church attendance was compulsory, by law, and the clergy clearly had a considerable influence over the people's moral values. If they probably failed to instil a deep theological understanding, they inculcated a sense of the awfulness of Popery—a service of thanksgiving for the failure of the Gunpowder Plot was added to the Prayer Book in 1662—and of the subject's duty to obey established authority. 'From all sedition, privy conspiracy and rebellion,' ran the litany, 'Good Lord deliver us.' From the pulpit parsons appealed for charity for galley-slaves or the victims of fire or Popish persecution. Occasionally, they were required to read government propaganda—for example James II's Declaration of Indulgence. On the whole, though, the clergy rarely spoke with a single political voice, except when urging obedience. More often they gave their own views, denouncing Whiggery or Toryism, Dissent or Popery. How much notice their parishioners took is impossible to say. Even when church attendance was supposedly compulsory, the laws were erratically enforced. From the time of James's indulgence people could stay away with impunity, either because they were Dissenters or Catholics, or because they simply did not want to go to church. Congregations dwindled. Even when a strong-minded squire drove his villagers to church, he could not force them to pay attention. Even so, it is clear that the pulpit (Anglican and Dissenting) was a powerful political force. The clergy were often active in politics and stirred their flocks to energetic and occasionally violent action, most spectacularly in the Sacheverell riots of 1710.

The pulpit, an oral medium, could, potentially, reach anyone. The press was primarily the medium of the literate, although there are many references to people reading newspapers and storybooks to their illiterate fellows. The measurement of literacy is a complex problem. One can measure ability to write, by seeing who could not sign his name, but an inability to write did not necessarily imply an inability to read. Whereas now children are taught reading and writing together, in the seventeenth century reading was taught first, from the age of about six. Many children started work at seven, so missed out on the chance of learning to write. Nevertheless, as we have no means of assessing how many people could read, the best that historians can do is to use the evidence of changes in the ability to write. David Cressy has shown that literacy levels improved substantially between the sixteenth and eighteenth centuries. In the 1520s only about ten per cent of men could sign their names; by 1640 the percentage had risen to thirty and by 1750 to sixty. The figure for women rose from virtually nil in the 1520s to ten per cent in 1640 and forty per cent in 1750. Predictably, literacy was very unevenly distributed. Towns boasted a higher level than villages and people of wealth and status were more likely to be literate than the poor and humble. Schooling cost money and poor families were the least able to do without the pittance which a child's labour would bring in. It would not, however, be true to say simply that the rich were literate and the poor were not. Craftsmen and shopkeepers who needed to order goods and transmit payments over a distance had greater need of literacy than village craftsmen who could find work and secure payment on a face-to-face basis: yet some of the latter (tanners, for example) could be wealthier than many of the former.

The pulpit was a potentially formidable medium of communication, but not all Anglican parsons succeeded in stimulating their congregations. 'The Sleeping Congregation' by William Hogarth, engraved by C. Armstrong, 1736. The Mansell Collection

Moreover, many very poor people did, somehow, manage to learn to read and write. The large number of village schools, and of teachers, shows a vigorous demand for basic education. Many parents, then as now, made sacrifices to give their offspring a good start in life—or access to the Bible. Some achieved literacy only as adults. Thomas Tryon was taught to read by a fellow-shepherd, but as his colleague could not write, Tryon sought out a lame schoolmaster, offering a sheep as payment.

In the period around 1688, then, literacy was growing, but remained strongest in towns (especially London) and among the better off. Ability to read, however, did not necessarily imply an interest in political literature, assuming that such literature was available. The best-sellers of later Stuart England were almanacs and 'pleasant histories'—thrillers and romances. However, some political publications attracted wide interest: Henry Sacheverell's polemical sermon, *The Perils of False Brethren*, sold nearly one hundred thousand copies in 1709–10. Clearly there was a market for political literature—if writers and publishers could tap it.

The 1640s had seen an explosion of political publishing—pamphlets, petitions to Parliament, news-sheets and newspapers. At the Restoration censorship was reimposed. All works intended for publication had to be submitted to a secretary of state or senior churchman for licensing: to publish unlicensed works was to risk severe punishment. This legislation became largely inoperable after the Revolution and lapsed in 1695, but the press was not now totally free. Attacks on the government could lead to prosecution for seditious libel. Stamp taxes on printed material pushed up the price of pamphlets and newspapers to a level which poorer people could not afford. Parliament tried, as late as the 1760s, to prevent publication of its debates. Nevertheless, political publications flourished. National and provincial newspapers grew in numbers and confidence. Parliamentary reporting developed, if somewhat precariously, using subterfuges, such as giving MPs easily recognisable fictitious names or delaying publication until after the end of the session. During the long ministry of Sir Robert Walpole (1721–42) he was attacked in the press with a persistence and venom which amazed foreigners used to more authoritarian regimes. Although Walpole tried to muzzle his more outspoken attackers—he introduced censorship of stage-plays, by the lord chamberlain—he lacked the power to silence all criticism and countered it through the sponsorship of pro-ministerial publications, further increasing the amount of political literature put before the public.

It is difficult to assess the readership of eighteenth-century newspapers. *The Craftsman*, in the 1730s, had a peak print run of 13,000; the London newspapers together were estimated to print 30,000 to 50,000 copies a week. Provincial newspapers, which often pirated items from those of London, were produced on a smaller scale, but by the 1760s the largest sold 2,000. (Walpole's *Daily Gazetteer* sold only about 1,000, with another 2,000 given away.) Such figures would suggest that the press reached only a small fraction of the population, which even in 1688 numbered over five millions. Contemporaries insisted, however, that each copy was read many times: some said forty. This may have been true of the copies bought by taverns and coffee-houses, but many were bought by private subscribers, so were presumably read only by their families and by one or two friends. The nature of the distribution network limited the readership. In London and all but the smallest provincial towns, newspapers were available to anybody with the price of a cup of coffee or a mug of ale. Elsewhere, they would reach only those who could afford to have them posted to them, although some enterprising provincial newspaper proprietors organised deliveries well outside the town. Other forms of information, especially handwritten newsletters, were still more expensive and so socially exclusive. William Cobbett wrote of his upbringing in rural Surrey:

> As to politics, we were like the rest of the country people in England: that is to say we neither knew nor cared anything about the matter . . . I do not remember ever having seen a newspaper in the house and most certainly that privation . . . did not render us less free, happy or industrious.

Thus, when it came to the dissemination of political information, the big difference was not between rich and poor, but between town and country. In larger towns, especially London, political debate embraced most ranks of society: in rural areas it was confined mainly to a narrow elite. When it came to participation in local government, differences between town and country were less marked. In both, the higher levels were the preserve of the better off. County government was dominated by Justices of the Peace, both magistrates and administrators, and by the lord lieutenant and his deputies, who commanded the militia. Both were recruited from among the nobility and upper gentry, although from the later seventeenth century it became increasingly difficult to involve the greatest county figures in the humdrum details of petty crime and poor relief. The bulk of the work was therefore done by lesser gentlemen, clergymen and even (in London and its environs) paid magistrates. The nature of county office—unpaid, time-consuming and increasingly complex—ensured that only the wealthiest elements in society could take it on. Working farmers could not spare the time, did not have the necessary education and lacked the natural authority which came with rank and inherited wealth.

In the towns the picture was similar. Most were ruled by corporations which were nominally elected, but filled vacancies by some disguised form of co-option. Municipal offices were filled by the richer (and often more elderly) members of the business community (plus a few lawyers), because they alone had the leisure and the income to take on civic responsibilities. Being an alderman was prestigious, but expensive: one was expected to contribute to municipal loans and charities and to entertain visiting dignitaries. Office was seen as a burden and some preferred to pay a large fine rather than accept it. Thus many towns came to be ruled by inter-related groups of well-heeled families.

One might think that the rule of such narrow elites would provoke resentment. Sometimes it did, but usually it did not, for three reasons. First, it had always been that way and this society rarely questioned traditional ways of doing things; also, respect for rank ran deep, especially in rural areas. Second, much of the business of local government had little impact on the individual. Even now, turnout in local elections is low and in the seventeenth century even the London common council elections usually aroused little interest. Third, at the level which most affected the average person, there was a large measure of participation. In London most householders held ward or parish offices from time to time, perhaps as often as one year in three. Each ward had an 'Inquest', a jury which supervised a wide range of commercial, moral and environmental matters—and demanded action when things went wrong. The lives of rural parishes, too, were regulated by parishioners, as churchwardens, overseers of the poor and constables. Many had manorial courts, where disputes were adjudicated by the villagers themselves, while hundred and county grand juries told the JPs what needed to be done. From all these responsibilities the poorest inhabitants were usually excluded, as they lacked the respect of their fellows and sufficient literacy and numeracy to keep records and accounts. Even so, the level of participation was high, which helped to create a widely diffused knowledge of the law and understanding of the basic processes of government. Yeomen and village craftsmen might not keep up with the latest political news from London, or the continent, but many had definite views about their legal rights and the proper functioning of government.

If people of different ranks participated in government, they did not do so on equal terms, for English society was profoundly unequal. This did not necessarily mean that it was deeply divided. Deference to rank and authority was deep-rooted and was reinforced by the Church's teachings, which made acceptance of the status quo a Christian duty. Inequality

----

(Right) *James II, a king undone by a combination of his own flaws of character and bad luck. From the painting by Kneller.* By courtesy of the National Portrait Gallery, London

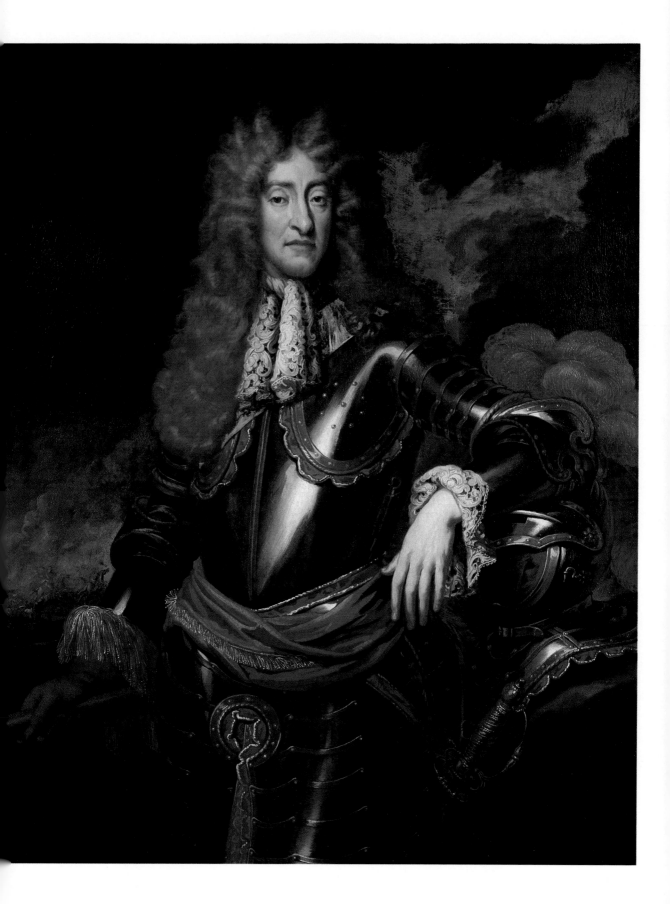

did not always breed envy: the humble might enjoy vicariously the pampered lifestyle of the rich—stately homes were first opened to the public in the eighteenth century—and prosperous bourgeois tried to emulate and ultimately join the landed elite. Fortunes made in trade or the law were invested in country estates and conspicuous consumption: there came a point where *arrivistes* craved status more than profit. They married their daughters to the sons of peers and baronets and sent their sons to prestigious public schools to acquire the manners and the contacts they would need to make their way in aristocratic society. It took several generations of hard graft for those born outside the landowning classes to claw their way into the peerage: no merchant managed it in the eighteenth century. Below the nobility, however, there was greater mobility, enabling the landed elite to absorb, and stamp its values upon, ambitious and successful men from humbler backgrounds.

The development of a coherent ruling elite was made easier by the emergence of London as *the* centre of aristocratic social life. The royal court, the law courts, the more regular meetings of Parliament—all helped to draw provincial landowners to the capital. New squares and streets were built in the West End to house them, new services and places of leisure sprang up to cater for their every need. Squires from Cornwall mingled with those from Cumberland or Cambridgeshire, regional differences were subsumed in a common metropolitan culture: leisured, polite and fashionable. Overt provincialism came to be seen as uncouth: the manners of society's leaders were aped by all who wished to be regarded as 'the quality'.

The styles and fashions of London were transmitted into the provinces, via newspapers, fashion magazines and what one might call the outstations of London society—the spas and large provincial towns. Bath under Beau Nash offered a model of ordered, polite living, with the day regulated by the clock and no dancing after eleven at night—even for royalty. Tunbridge Wells, once notorious for its debauchery, followed Nash's lead, becoming a 'rendezvous for gaiety and politeness'. More and more provincial towns built assembly rooms, theatres, concert halls and circulating

––––––––––––

(Above left) *John Locke's* Second Treatise of Government *set out a view of the Revolution as the expulsion, by the people, of a tyrant, which found wider acceptance in later generations than in his own time. After a painting by Kneller, c. 1704.* By courtesy of the National Portrait Gallery, London

(Left) *Although lawyers were often caricatured as bloated and corrupt, England's system of criminal justice was among the fairest in eighteenth-century Europe. 'The Bench' by William Hogarth.* Reproduced by permission of the Syndics of the Fitzwilliam Museum, Cambridge

Beau Nash created at Bath a form of 'polite' social life, entry to which depended not only on wealth but also on a willingness to observe carefully defined standards of dress and behaviour. Statue by Joseph Plura. By courtesy of the Victoria Art Gallery, Bath

The mannered elegance of Bath was one example of a growing separation between 'polite' society and the rougher, more spontaneous amusements of the poor. View of the North Parade, Bath, by Thomas Malton, c. 1777. Bath Reference Library

libraries, so that they too could enjoy the pleasures and cultural pursuits of London. A fashion developed for 'lectures upon the arts and sciences, superficial enough to entertain the imagination without fatiguing the understanding'. Meetings for county business, like the assizes, provided an occasion for balls and other entertainments for the cream of society.

In some ways, the growth of 'politeness' brought people together. Nash insisted that anyone with reasonable means and decent clothes could enjoy the delights of Bath: charges to use the walks varied according to rank. At Tunbridge Wells 'the social virtues reign triumphant over prejudice ... deists and Christians, Whigs and Tories, Scots and English debate without anger, dispute with politeness and judge with candour.' It had long been noted that in England a 'gentleman' was defined less by birth than by dress and demeanour, but those who lacked education and money could never hope to break into polite society. The more mannered and self-consciously fashionable that society became, the more its members became distinct from their humbler neighbours and tenants. In Glamorgan, a linguistic gulf opened between the Welsh-speaking peasantry and the English-speaking gentry. In town and county, elites distanced themselves

51

To sweetscented Sirs who are sick of the Sport, *GREENWICH HILL* — There heighten'd with Raptures, which never can pall,
And the stale languid Follies of Ball-room or Court, *or Holyday Gambols.* Youl own, the Delights of Assembly and Ball
For a change leave the Mall to Greenwich resort. Are as dull as Yourselves & just nothing at all.

THE SORTS AND CONDITIONS OF MEN

from the common herd, in assembly rooms and enclosed walks; stands were built at race-courses, for which tickets were required. Sometimes efforts at segregation proved ineffectual. Attempts to exclude the poor and scruffy from royal parks in London failed lamentably—Londoners were notoriously insubordinate—and, in the theatre, reserving seats in the pit for well-to-do left them at the mercy of those in the cheap seats in the gallery. Nevertheless, as the eighteenth century wore on, polite society became less willing to patronise, or tolerate, rough plebeian entertainment. Violence against people or animals slowly became unfashionable. Aristocrats became less likely to give their patronage to contests between men (and sometimes women), using fists, staves or swords, in which the participants would occasionally stop to have their wounds stitched before fighting on. Town councils no longer countenanced cock-throwing, bear-baiting, bull-running or even the Dunmow Flitch (a side of bacon presented to the most happily married couple in the town). Civic ceremonies came to revolve around the corporation, with the townspeople reduced to mere spectators.

How far such changes weakened the cohesion of society one cannot tell. It seems likely, however, that a landowner who spent much of his time in London or Bath, who took a limited personal interest in his estates, who rarely dispensed hospitality in person, who played no part in local government and who could perhaps not even speak his tenants' language, would command only limited loyalty from his inferiors. However, those who could afford to dissociate themselves from their locality to this extent were comparatively few. Multitudes of lesser gentry remained (for better or worse) in close contact with their tenants and labourers and played an active part in local government. In towns, although leading burgher families tried to distance themselves from the townspeople, most lived in too close proximity to them to do so completely. The sinews holding society together may at times have come under increasing strain in the century after 1688, but they seldom seemed likely to snap.

(Top left) *In assembly rooms, civic leaders and provincial gentry imitated the social and intellectual styles of London, while excluding the poor and vulgar. The Assembly Rooms at Bury St Edmunds, Suffolk, opened about 1713, and renamed the Athenaeum in 1854.* Suffolk County Council

(Left) *Not all places of pleasure were socially exclusive: at Greenwich and in London's parks, both rich and poor could disport themselves. 'Greenwich Hill or Holyday Gambols', a satirical engraving of 1750.* Greenwich Local History Library

CHAPTER FOUR

THE PEOPLE AND THE REVOLUTION

The Revolution of 1688 is often seen as a 'respectable revolution': an aristocratic putsch in which lesser folk played no real part. That was how the ruling elite wished it to be and how it was later represented by both Whig and more radical historians. The former wished the keystone of the constitution to be free from the violence which tarnished the French Revolution. The latter assumed, because there was little violence, that it could not be a proper revolution: the 'real' English revolution, they argued, was that of 1640–60. As we have seen, the Revolution of 1688 has often been misunderstood or misrepresented. It would be unwise to take on trust bland assertions that 'the people' played no real part in it.

Seventeeth-century politics was rarely the exclusive preserve of the elite. Whatever the inequities of the electoral system, Parliament was a representative institution and MPs occasionally had to face the electors. Only a minority of seats were contested, but, in those that were, candidates found increasingly that the electors wished to know where they stood politically. The electors rarely put forward demands of their own, but when the elite was divided (as in 1640 or the Exclusion Crisis) the electors took a keen interest in the points at issue and took sides with a zeal that could embarrass the candidates. At Great Marlow in 1679 there were 'brave doings . . . breaking arms and legs and heads with stones'. One of the victorious candidates was ducked by a bargeman 'so under water that all cried to save him'. The more intense competition for seats became, the more Whig and Tory peers and gentlemen sought the support of the electorate and of the politically informed public; and, as we have seen, that public was far wider than the lucky few affluent enough to put themselves forward for election.

In short, disputes within the elite led to attempts to win the hearts and minds of the middling and lower sort, especially in the towns, which returned four-fifths of MPs and where political knowledge was greatest. Thus when James II began his campaign to pack Parliament, he used not only threats and chicanery but canvassing and propaganda, using techniques developed by those, who, less than a decade before, had wished to exclude him from the throne. The government-sponsored *Public Occurrences* was written by Henry Care, who had earlier produced a violently Whig history of Popery, in weekly parts. The aim of this and other government propaganda was to extol the benefits of toleration and persuade Dissenters that James's offer of religious freedom was not simply a cover for the advancement of Popery. Meanwhile, James tried to deny his opponents the means to express their views. The ecclesiastical commission tried to stop Anglican clergymen preaching against Popery and press censorship continued, under the Licensing Act. It was not very effective. Over two hundred anti-Catholic tracts appeared during the reign, but more worrying were overtly political works, which circulated clandestinely. 'This alliance between liberty and infallibility,' wrote the Marquis of Halifax in *A Letter to a Dissenter*, 'is bringing together the two most contrary things that are in the world. The Church of Rome doth not only dislike the allowing liberty, but by its principles it cannot do it . . . You are therefore,' he warned the Dissenters, 'to be hugged now only that you may be the better squeezed at another time.' In 1687–8 many pamphlets were sent over from Holland. *A Letter from Mijn Heer Fagel* assured Dissenters that William and Mary would grant toleration to all; they could therefore be sure of their liberty without making the concessions to Catholics which James demanded. Bogus letters from Jesuits claimed that James and Louis were plotting to eradicate Protestantism, while works with titles like *Idem Iterum, or the History of Queen Mary's Big-Belly* cast doubt on the queen's pregnancy.

Distributing this material was a complex operation. Some forty thousand copies of Fagel's *Letter* were printed. *A Letter to a Dissenter* was distributed simultaneously in different parts of the country, which made it harder to suppress. The pamphlets reinforced fears about James's intentions and doubts about his son's legitimacy. They helped to sustain an atmosphere of alarm in the last months of 1688, heightened by rumours of all kinds: Irish troops were landing in the north, the French were believed to be landing just about anywhere. When Feversham disbanded the army, the Irish regiments headed for home. News of their coming gave rise to waves of panic: thousands of bloodthirsty Papists were going to put all the Protestants to the sword. They were said to have burned Bedford, Birmingham and Stafford. News that they were approaching Lancashire led to more than four thousand men appearing to guard Warrington bridge. Similar alarums occurred as far apart as Berwick, Cornwall and Norfolk.

That a few hundred 'poor, naked, timorous and hated Irish', 'with scarce a knife to cut their victuals', should have caused such panic was due in part to the hiatus created by James's flight, but the atmosphere had been

A LETTER,

Writ by Mijn Heer F. A G E L,

PENSIONER of HOLLAND,

TO

Mr. JAMES STEWART, Advocate;

Giving an Account of the

PRINCE and PRINCESS

of O R A N G E's

Thoughts concerning *the Repeal* of the TEST, and the PENAL LAWS.

SIR,

I Am extream forry, that my ill health hath fo long hindred me from Anfwering thofe Letters, in which you fo earneftly defired to know of me, what Their *Highneffes* thoughts are, concerning the Repeal of the *Penal Laws*, and more particularly of that concerning the *Teft* : I beg you to affure your felf, that I will deal very plainly with you in this matter, and without Referve, fince you fay that your *Letters* were writ by the *King's* knowledge and allowance. I muft then *firft* of all affure you very pofitively, that Their *Highneffes* have often declared, as They did it more particularly to the Marquis of *Albeville*, His Majefties *Envoy* Extraordinary to the *States*, that it is Their Opinion, *that no Chriftian ought to be perfecuted for his Confcience, or be ill ufed becaufe he differs from the publick and eftablifhed Religion* ; And therefore, They can confent,

that

tense for some weeks. 'False rumours never more abounded in this nation, which causes the greater inflammation of the people'. That 'inflammation' was seen not in the pursuit of specifically 'popular' objectives, but in fear and hatred of Papists and in enthusiasm for William. William's declaration was widely disseminated, as was the spurious *Third Declaration of the Prince of Orange*, which stated that the Papists planned to put London to fire and sword and declared that all Catholics were to be disarmed: any found in arms, or in an office, were to be killed. Even before such declarations, which seemed to legitimate attacks on Catholics, there had been riots at Catholic chapels, in London and elsewhere. To open or to attend these chapels was illegal and they had remained unmolested thanks only to the king's protection. The London militia, the trained bands, proved unwilling or unable to disperse the rioters, so regular soldiers were called in. On 12 November they fired on a crowd of one thousand, burning 'massing stuff' at Clerkenwell. Several were killed and a coroner's jury returned a verdict of wilful murder, describing the rioters as 'loyal persons' who had gathered to apprehend priests who had said mass contrary to law. Later a grand jury found a true bill against one of James's generals for trying to protect priests.

Who were these rioters? Descriptions such as 'the rabble' and 'the mobile' do not tell us much. References to 'boys' or 'children' could mean apprentices—a large, volatile, literate and politically informed group, with a habit of rioting on public holidays. Most seventeenth- and eighteenth-century crowds, in fact, did not consist of the very poor, but of artisans, shopkeepers and, of course, apprentices. Riots with a political content were especially likely to include men of some substance, which may help explain the sympathy with which these rioters were viewed by juries, themselves composed of respectable citizens. The riots forced James to close the chapels; the more prescient Catholic ambassadors prepared to leave. Concern for the security of London made James delay leaving for the west until after 17 November—Elizabeth's accession day, often celebrated with anti-Catholic demonstrations. When he left, he had to leave several thousand troops to maintain order; the City trained bands were also on guard each night, to protect the citizens against the Papists. Late in November there were wild rumours that the lieutenant of the Tower, Sir Edward Hales, planned to bombard the City, after he moved mortars in: James dismissed him. On 7 December the Lord Mayor ordered that all

---

The press played a vital part in the Revolution, both in disseminating news and in the battle for hearts and minds. Fagel's Letter, *produced in Holland, was one of the most effective early salvoes in that battle.* By permission of the Syndics of Cambridge University Library

Papists should be disarmed: he had had little option—a delegation of citizens had told him that if he did not give the order, they would do it themselves.

How far the need to leave troops in London would have weakened James's army we shall never know, because it never came to blows. It is, however, clear that the mounting disorder and universal evidence of anti-Popery further undermined James's battered morale. His people hated him and the anti-Catholic rioting raised ugly memories of the outbreak of the civil war. The attitude of William and his followers was ambivalent. William had had no qualms about exploiting popular violence when it suited him, but he knew that, once unleashed, it could be hard to control: for this reason he disavowed the *Third Declaration*. Those who rose on his behalf in the north were mostly careful not to assert a right of resistance, which might be used to challenge aristocratic rule. Danby seized York on the pretext that the Papists were about to rise. Others called for a free Parliament, claiming to defend 'the Protestant religion, our laws and liberties and the ancient constitution'. The Tory peers who escorted Anne to Nottingham stressed that only concern for her safety led them to take up arms. Even the Whig peers recruited first and foremost among their, and their neighbours', tenants: they did not issue a general summons. Lord Delamere made no bones about claiming a right of resistance, but rejected offers from the 'ordinary sort' to serve him: William, he said, had all the infantry he needed.

However, alarmist rumours of French invasion and Popish insurrection and more solid news of William's activities created a popular interest and involvement which were not easily contained: in London, it was pressure from below which drove the Lord Mayor to order the disarming of the Catholics. Thirty of the 'rabble' seized Dover castle, despite the mayor's efforts to dissuade them. At Ashford the townspeople were angry that the gentry failed to appear and declare for William, at a time of so much danger. At Carlisle the people were so restive that the governor confiscated all possible weapons and trained his cannon on the town. When James fled, on the 10th, things threatened to get out of hand. In London, Catholic chapels were rased to the ground and the Spanish ambassador's house was gutted and looted; newly disbanded soldiers were among the rioters. A committee of peers met at the Guildhall and tried to restore order, but there seemed to be riots everywhere. The next night, fear that the Irish were coming distracted the Londoners from rioting, but they stayed awake all night, firing muskets and banging pots and pans, presumably to frighten the Irish off.

These disorders strengthened William's hand: 'everybody is in great frights and wish for the Prince of Orange's coming, to quiet things'. He sent word that he wanted the disorders stopped and that ambassadors' property was to be protected. The peers at Guildhall did what they could, but it was a moot point where real authority lay and this, together with the Irish panic, led people to take the law into their own hands. Everywhere the watch, or vigilante bands, kept a lookout for priests. Many priests and foreigners were arrested, as were others (like Judge Jeffreys) associated with James's regime; some were also robbed. James himself was taken, in disguise, off the Isle of Sheppey. His captors called him an 'ugly, lean-jawed, hatchet-faced Jesuit' and subjected him to a humiliating search 'even to his privities'. The seamen refused to hand over their captives to the local gentry and eventually let James return to London with the greatest reluctance, even threatening to fight Feversham's guards.

All over the country Catholic chapels and homes were attacked and Catholics were assaulted and plundered. Although the crowds formed in towns, they often went far into the countryside if they heard of stocks of powder and arms in Catholic mansions. Crowds from Cambridge and Bury St Edmunds marched to Lord Dover's house at Cheveley, demolished his chapel, ripped up hangings to make scarves and slaughtered his deer. The people of Bury assembled in such numbers that the local militia could not disperse them. They burned the goods of the town's few Catholics, ripping up feather beds and giving 'superabundant testimony of the ill consequence of a popular fury': the women were especially violent. Later, on news that the Irish were coming, a crowd of some five hundred, styling themselves 'the Protestant reformers', rambled around demanding money for 'taxes' and plundering Catholic and Protestant alike. The militia, when ordered to fire on them, laid down their arms and forced their colonel to declare for 'free booty', so some two hundred gentlemen and townsmen took up arms and suppressed them.

Defiance and indiscriminate disorder, like that at Bury, were unusual and did not last long. When a 'mob' near Norwich ignored the commands of the magistrates and militia, many were whipped and imprisoned. Usually crowds concentrated their attacks on Catholics: tradesmen with shop-signs like the 'pope's head' hastily took them down. A crowd which assembled outside the papal nuncio's house in London moved on when his land-lord assured them that he had gone. Often men of rank and authority could calm fears and make people hand back what they had stolen. At Gloucester, Mr Cook, a magistrate, secured the return of most of what had been taken from the Catholics and then agreed to become mayor. Often Catholics' goods were burned, to show that this was a legitimate act of punishment, and not simple theft. When James's captors refused to hand him over to the gentlemen, it was partly because they feared that the latter would take all the credit, partly because they felt that some of the gentry were insufficiently committed to William and partly (so they later claimed) because they were concerned for James's safety. Despite alarmist comments from members of the elite, seventeenth-century riots were rarely indiscriminate or innately hostile to authority. Rioters usually felt that their actions were legitimated by law and justice—in this case, they believed that what James had done in favour of Catholics was illegal—and they were often swayed by fear. They could therefore be appeased by trusted members of the elite, provided these took the steps which the rioters regarded as necessary.

For a few days, just before and just after James's first flight, it seemed to some that the 'mob ruled all' and could have been the masters 'if the beasts had known their own strength'. That, however, assumed a degree of social conflict which did not exist in Stuart England. As the Earl of Ailesbury rode to bring James back to London, in each town and village he calmed the fears of humble men and women, terrified that the Irish were coming. He wrote later:

> I cannot say enough in praise of the goodness of our populace and of the contrary of them of Holland and Flanders, and I should have been very sorry to have been amongst them as I was now surrounded with my countrymen: for with these 'tis like a fire of straw—soon lighted and as soon quenched.

More typical than the disorderly scenes at Bury and Norwich was that at King's Lynn. The corporation waited upon the Duke of Norfolk in the market place and prayed him to stand by them in defence of their liberties and the Protestant religion. Many came to offer their services and he was afterwards entertained to a great dinner. Deference and subordination were rarely threatened in 1688, partly because the elite acted quickly to reimpose its authority, but more because the lower orders never seriously sought to challenge that authority. Even James, unpopular though he was, was treated with respect once his captors realised that he was not a Jesuit and especially after he had washed and shaved and was dressed like a king. When he returned to London large crowds cheered him, although their cheers perhaps owed more to sympathy than to enthusiasm.

When William came to London, on 18 December, government quickly returned to normal. There was a flurry of political publishing: at least five different newspapers appeared in the course of the month, although most soon ceased publication. In the election campaign of January 1689, it seems that, while the usual electoral tricks were employed and the Whigs used the Association to embarrass the Tories, this was (by the standards of the time) a free and fair election: William moved his troops out of the parliamentary boroughs while it was going on. By now, the time for direct popular action had passed: 'the people' were once more to exercise their influence through the restricted channel of the hustings. When some who wished to offer William and Mary the crown incited 'the mobile, who came in a tumultuous manner with a petition', both Houses refused to receive it. Nevertheless, this incident, reviving memories of December, may have persuaded some Tories to accept William's regime: as one earl put it: 'We must not leave ourselves to the rabble.'

As the Revolution receded into the past, the Whig establishment quietly forgot the contribution made by popular disorder. Indeed, as aristocratic rule was threatened by late eighteenth-century radicalism, the Whigs denied that direct popular intervention had any legitimate role in politics and reassuringly portrayed 1688 as having secured the liberties of all ranks of Englishmen. Yet if 'the people' played an important role in 1688, they had not pursued distinct objectives of their own and there is little evidence that they were dissatisfied with the outcome. They had been saved from Popery and the Irish, their ancient liberties were secured, 'freeborn English-men' would remain free. They had not challenged aristocratic rule and so were not disappointed that it continued. The fact that England's government remained aristocratic after 1688 did not make it an 'aristocratic' revolution. Nor did most English people see it that way, because the elite's interests were not seen as different from, or opposed to, those of society as a whole.

CHAPTER FIVE

THE REVOLUTION AND THE STATE

One great irony of seventeenth-century English history is that both the Parliamentarians of the 1640s and the makers of the Revolution of 1688 sought to curb what they saw as a dangerous growth of royal power; in each case, their actions led to a major strengthening of the State. By 1714 taxation was far heavier and the State's means of coercion were more effective than they had been in the reign of James I. Yet the English continued to regard themselves as a free people, a view widely echoed by visitors from abroad. How can one explain this?

James I inherited a ramshackle fiscal system, based on three main sources of revenue. First, the personal resources of the monarch—Crown lands (which were gradually sold off) and feudal rights. Second, customs duties, which Parliament normally granted to each monarch for life, at his accession. Third, subsidies: taxes on land, voted on an *ad hoc* basis, when the king could persuade Parliament that they were needed. Subsidies could take several years to collect and were plagued by chronic under-assessment. As James I and Charles I were often not on good terms with Parliament, they found it hard to raise as much as they needed, especially as prices were rising. It was, in short, a muddled, archaic system. With no permanent, accurately assessed tax on land, the main source of wealth went largely untaxed. The system's one great merit was that the poorest people were effectively exempt from taxation.

This changed in the 1640s. The king's feudal rights were abolished. Needing to raise large sums quickly to carry on the civil war, Parliament for the first time had to grapple constructively with the problem of taxation. It developed the monthly (or weekly) assessment, whereby each county and town had to produce a set sum by a specified time. This was far quicker and was levied at a far heavier rate than the subsidy. It also introduced the excise, a tax on certain commodities (mostly alcoholic drinks) produced and consumed within England. This fell disproportionately heavily on the poor—bread and beer were the staples of the working man's diet. As brewing was a cottage industry, excisemen demanded entry

THE REVOLUTION AND THE STATE

into people's homes, to check how much they were brewing. Both devices, but particularly the excise, were bitterly hated, but Parliament, unlike the early Stuarts, had an army and no qualms about using it against obstinate taxpayers. By 1660 the English (not least the poor) were getting used to paying heavy, regular taxes.

Charles II's reign saw some relief for the taxpayer. In the 1660s the Commons voted far larger sums for war than their early Stuart predecessors, but thereafter Charles's problems with Parliament ensured that little direct taxation was granted. The early enthusiasm of the 1685 Parliament meant that James II's revenue reached the dizzy heights of two million pounds a year—double that of his father. But this was to seem paltry compared with what came later.

When William invaded England, France was already at war with the Dutch, Spain and the Emperor. James fled to France, Louis pledged to restore him to his throne: if James was not to return as a French puppet, England had to join the war. Both Whigs and Tories were agreed on the need for war: as in the 1640s Parliament was committed to a war of self-preservation, for which very large amounts of money had to be raised very quickly. A land-tax was established at a notional rate of four shillings in the pound. Levels of assessment soon ossified, so that yields came to seem less than adequate, but in the 1690s a yield approaching £2,000,000 a year seemed very large—almost as much as James II's revenue from all sources. The effort was all the greater as farm prices were far from buoyant, so that landlord and tenant alike struggled to raise the money. For this reason, the Commons involved the leading gentry of each county in its assessment and collection. They might do the job less efficiently than the professionals who now collected the customs and excise, but the political benefits from mollifying the gentry outweighed any disadvantages.

The land-tax alone was not enough. A tax on non-landed income was beyond the resource of seventeenth-century bureaucracy and would have been bitterly resisted by the political and financial establishment as 'an inquisition more intolerable than any tax'. So the government looked elsewhere for substantial and reliable sources of revenue, not only to spend on the war, but also to provide sound security for loans. Some could come from import duties, but trade was disrupted in wartime, so the safest method was to add new excises to old. Although proposals for a general excise were rejected, new duties were placed on more and more commodities in the century after 1688. The burden of taxation went up by leaps and bounds. Charles II's revenue from taxation averaged less than £1,500,000 a year, to which the excise contributed less than £350,000. Between 1689 and 1713 the average revenue was over £4,400,000, with the average contribution of the excise almost £1,300,000. In the 1730s excises contributed almost exactly half of an average revenue of £5,750,000. By 1786–90 the average revenue had soared to over £16,000,000, with over £7,000,000 from the excise. Even allowing for the growth of population and prosperity and (in the later eighteenth century) the reappearance of inflation, it is clear that the tax burden (especially that on the poor) rose substantially.

It was not only taxation that increased. As wars became larger and more expensive, far more money was raised by borrowing. With interest rates as low as two per cent in the mid eighteenth century, huge sums could be borrowed cheaply. Borrowing was cheap partly because prices were stable in the first half of the century, but more because the government's credit was so good. Lending to kings was a risky business: repayments were tardy, they sometimes sought to renegotiate the terms of their loans and they might default altogether. For these reasons, lenders demanded high rates of interest: the average paid by Louis XIII of France in the 1630s was at least twenty-four per cent. After 1688, the Crown's credit was underpinned by that of Parliament. Kings were a bad risk not so much because they were financially feckless (though some were) but because they lacked ready money. Taxes secured by Acts of Parliament (notably excises) provided rock-solid security for wary investors, in England and abroad.

Before 1688 the Crown's credit had largely depended on that of private financiers, men who could persuade lenders to trust them with their money and then lent it to the king. Often they over-extended themselves and went bankrupt. One who did not was the remarkable Sir Stephen Fox, who rose from a humble office in the royal household to be 'the richest commoner in three kingdoms'. Unusual in his reputation for honesty, Fox received advances from earls, bishops and merchants; his credit alone kept Charles II afloat financially in the Exclusion Crisis. After 1688, however, the sums needed became too great even for Fox. Institutions were needed to link the investors and the government. Existing joint-stock trading companies (notably the East India Company) met this need to some extent, but increasingly a central role was played by the Bank of England. Established in 1694, it was empowered to deal in bills of exchange—the main method of transmitting money in the seventeenth century. The Bank's promissory notes came to be accepted as legal tender, reducing the need to rely on gold and silver coins. The Bank's ability to raise loans for the government gave it a considerable—some said a sinister—political influence: it wished to ensure that investors' money was not misused.

The growth of government borrowing after 1688 meant that eighteenth-century England became accustomed to deficit finance. In the great wars with France of 1689–97 and 1702–13, almost £46,000,000 was raised by loans. By 1714 the national debt stood at over £40,000,000,

In many Parliamentary boroughs in the eighteenth century, a small number of electors
would be lavishly entertained by the candidates . . . From Hogarth's *An Election*:
no.1 'An Election Entertainment'. *By courtesy of the Trustees of*
Sir John Soane's Museum

The moment of reckoning came when the electors had to give their votes, in public, watched by employers, landlords and often partisan crowds. From Hogarth's *An Election*: no.3 'The Polling'. *By courtesy of the Trustees of Sir John Soane's Museum*

with an annual interest charge of £2,520,000—more than James II's total annual revenue. Further wars brought further borrowing: in the French wars of 1793–1815 loans totalled £440,000,000. The national debt, which began as a direct result of the Revolution, was by the late eighteenth century absorbing as much as forty per cent of the government's revenue.

The huge increases in taxation and borrowing had several important effects. First, the administration became far larger. Until the 1680s the Crown employed few professional administrators and virtually none outside central departments, like the Exchequer. Local government was run almost entirely by amateurs. The 1670s and 1680s saw the creation of a network of customs and excise officers, but this growth was dwarfed by that after 1688. With the French wars, the armed forces, the departments responsible for their administration and the revenue service all expanded. As the State employed more people, the cost of government rose even higher and the volume of government patronage grew. In order to secure the co-operation of the dominant elements in society, the Crown needed to offer rewards, such as jobs, pensions and economic privileges. Before 1688 the Crown's revenue and patronage were both limited. After the Revolution, it had far more rewards at its disposal, which it could use to influence elections and to buy support in Parliament.

While the fiscal changes brought about by the Revolution created more jobs for the clients and kin of the ruling elite, the growth of government borrowing provided its members with secure and profitable investments. Although the landed classes disdained industry (as essentially artisanal) and rarely became personally involved in trade, they had a shrewd eye for a lucrative investment. Links between the landed elite and high finance were multifarious. In the City, trust was more important than resources and a gentlemanly code of honour developed which prevailed until very recently. Banks were family concerns, not vast impersonal corporations, so personal contacts and reputations were vital to a financier's credit. This common code of behaviour and these personal contacts were reinforced by intermarriage and education at the public schools. Bankers and landowners also shared a taste for conspicuous consumption: for the former, it also served the practical purpose of showing that they were men of substance.

The growth of government patronage and borrowing bound the ruling elite more and more closely to the post-Revolution order. Members of the elite wanted commissions in the army for their younger sons and places in the revenue service for clients and political supporters; they also invested profitably in the national debt. Meanwhile, the proportion of taxation paid by the rich declined, until income tax was introduced (amid squeals of outrage) in 1799. It would not be unduly cynical to see the eighteenth-century fiscal system as redistributing resources from the

A Booke

Conteyning the Subscriptions of such persons Natives and fforreigners, Bodies Politik and Corporate who voluntarily subscribe toward the raising and paying into the Receipt of Exchequer the Summe of twelve hundred thousand pounds pursuant to a Comission under the Great Seale of England Dated the fifteenth day of June Anno Dom 1694 grounded upon an Act of Parliament Entituled An Act for granting to their Ma:ties severall Rates and Duties upon Tunnage of Ships and Vessells and upon Beere Ale and other Liquors for securing certaine Recompences and Advantages in the said Act menconed to such persons as shall voluntarily advance ye summe of fifteene hundred thousand pounds towards the carrying on the War against France. In which Booke are conteyned the names of the severall persons Subscribing and the particular Summes of money Subscribed which Summes so Subscribed are sett against the respective Names of the severall persons Bodies Politik and Corporate subscribing and therein particularly named

Wee hereafter written in pursuance of the Act of Parliament and Comission above menconed Doe subscribe the severall Summes in this Booke set against our respective names in maner following viz:

London the 21:th day of June 1694

N.o 44 Wee Sydney Lord Godolphin Jo: Ha: Chd: Montague Will: Trumball Chr: ffitch Comrs of their Matie Treary doe Subscribe to and for the use & benefitt of their Ma:ties The Sum of Tenn Thousand Pounds

O:ex: Edgworth

poorer sections of society to the better-off. The impact of this redistribution was softened by the growing prosperity of the middling, and many of the lower, ranks of society, especially in the first half of the century, but it still occurred and it was resented. A verse of the early nineteenth century compared the symbols of high and low life in London, St James's and St Giles, and concluded that, morally, there was little to choose between a parasitic aristocracy and the criminal poor:

> Two places there are where the poor and the rich
> Live so like each other there's no knowing which . . .
> In the former they live on the national debt:
> In the latter they live on what they can get.

Eighteenth-century commentators often compared England with France. In England, they said, people grew fat on beef and beer; in France, half-starved peasants subsisted on onions and *soupe maigre*. This, they said, showed how much English 'freedom' was preferable to French 'slavery'. In fact, the disparity between taxation levels in the two countries was far less than contemporaries believed. By the late eighteenth century, the amount of money per head reaching the treasury was markedly less in France than in England (although the French fiscal system was so inefficient that what the average taxpayer paid may have been more nearly the same). Although the nobility and many other wealthy Frenchmen were exempt from some forms of taxation, they derived limited economic benefit from these privileges, as they had to accept reduced rents from their more heavily taxed tenants. Besides, although they had no formal fiscal privileges, the rich in England managed to pay proportionately less and less as the century advanced. In both countries, the aristocracy profited from the State's fiscal and credit systems. In France, government offices (especially revenue offices) were more attractive investments than trade or industry: in both countries the rich and powerful invested heavily in the king's debts.

One final result of the growth of taxation after 1688 was to add to the problems of the small farmer. Squeezed by falling profits and rising taxes, many went out of business. Landlords sought to sustain or increase their incomes by encouraging tenants to become more productive and profitable. They leased out land in larger units to more substantial tenants

---

A list of early subscribers to the Bank of England. Subscribers not only made a financial investment but showed their faith in the permanence (and creditworthiness) of the post-Revolution regime. By courtesy of the Governor and Company of the Bank of England

with the capital to undertake improvements. Often this required the redistribution of all the land in a village, through a private Act of Parliament, which often also deprived landless labourers of their surviving common rights. In general the gulf in arable villages between the few wealthy farmers and the many landless labourers became even greater in the eighteenth century, but this redistribution of lands also opened the way for more efficient agriculture and for spectacular increases in productivity. This owed something to the rationalisation of farms, but more to the adoption of new techniques, many originating in the Low Countries. New crop rotations (including fodder crops like turnips and sainfoin) removed the need to leave land fallow every third or fourth year and allowed those engaged in mixed husbandry to keep more beasts through the winter, accumulating more manure to enrich the fields the next year. In the century before 1660 farm prices and profits had been high and farmers had seen little need to make changes. In the much more unfavourable economic conditions after 1660 farmers were forced to adopt these new techniques or go out of business. The new taxes after 1688 can only have accelerated this development.

If the revenue system and the tax burden grew after 1688, so did the army. Long distrusted as an instrument of tyranny, a peacetime standing army became the norm after 1714. The army had served England well in the long wars of 1689–1713 and still seemed necessary to the Whig establishment in the face of the continued threat of Jacobitism. In the aftermath of the Jacobite rising of 1715, Parliament passed the Riot Act. This attempted to clarify the law by allowing soldiers to fire on rioters who failed to disperse within an hour of being required to by a person in authority. However, magistrates and politicians remained reluctant to use the military—some claimed that they could not fire until the hour was up—and army officers were reluctant to intervene. They had no wish to make war on civilians and feared repercussions if they did. 'From the nature of our constitution,' it was remarked, 'the civil power will always in disputes (unless on very extraordinary occasions) have the advantage of the military.'

Thus while the State now possessed a more effective instrument of coercion, engrained public hostility made ministers chary of using it. The English continued to rely on the navy to protect their shores and their empire (which did not prevent the government from scandalously underfunding it). Soldiers were unpopular and undervalued: a former Secretary at War declared, 'I hope, sir, that we have men enough in Great Britain who have resolution enough to defend themselves against any invasion whatsoever, though there were not so much as one redcoat in the whole kingdom.' Yet when the government tried to create an alternative force, by reinvigorating the militia, it met with apathy and antagonism: it took twenty years to turn it into a viable force. Despite their fondness for fighting one another, the English remained strongly anti-militaristic. Even so, the army survived and helped make England a European and world power, as well as providing a career for the sons of the nobility and gentry.

In local government, the Revolution changed very little. Except on matters of revenue and public order, central government allowed local officials to govern as they saw fit. It no longer tried to make them enforce traditional regulations on the marketing of grain, designed to protect the consumer. Now that economic conditions no longer favoured farmers and landlords, Parliament showed more concern for producers, paying bounties on grain exports in order to prevent a glut (and rock-bottom prices) at home. Local governors, then, were left to cope with new problems as best they could. It was typical that a major shift in policy towards poor relief took place following a decision by some Berkshire JPs at an inn at Speenhamland in 1795: decision-making was decentralised. Town councils responded to problems of urban growth in an improvised manner, setting up lighting, paving and cleansing commissions and raising the money by local rates. Road transport was improved by turnpike trusts, water transport by canal companies—in each case, the impetus came from local private initiatives and the promoters recouped their investment by charging tolls to users. Central government contributed little, except that Parliament's lengthy, regular meetings made it far easier for individuals, syndicates and town councils to plan and promote a piece of legislation. Far more local and private Acts—for enclosures, turnpikes, *ad hoc* bodies— were passed than ever before. The eighteenth century thus saw the extension of the tradition that the localities should govern themselves, which had been vindicated in 1688 after the intrusive policies of James II.

The Revolution was also seen as having preserved the law. The judiciary was freed from the crude political pressures to which it had been subjected in the 1680s, and especially by James. In 1701 it was laid down that judges could be dismissed only at the request of Parliament, but that did not make them immune from politics. They were appointed by politicians and during the long period of Whig rule after 1714 they naturally reflected the political views of the government. This was seen in prosecutions of the authors and publishers of oppositionist literature and, still more, in the 'Jacobin trials' of the 1790s, as the establishment closed ranks against the threat of revolution. The judges did not, however, slavishly support the government. Ministers' attempts to silence John Wilkes, in 1763–5, were impeded by adverse rulings from the judges. Moreover, if the judges supported the government, juries might ignore their advice: the days when judges could imprison jurors for giving the 'wrong' verdict had passed.

In general, England's legal system after 1688 probably protected individual liberty and political freedom better than any other in Europe:

William III was disgusted to find that torture was illegal. The law might be slow and costly, eccentric and over-technical, but it was (by the standards of the day) relatively impartial and generally respected. One reason for this was that relatively humble people were involved in its enforcement. On the continent, criminal prosecutions were usually instigated by professional judges, with a financial interest in bringing as many cases as possible to court. In England the initiative lay with the victim, or his kin. The cost and disruption involved encouraged people to avoid prosecuting where possible. Many minor transgressions were forgiven, many interpersonal disputes were settled by arbitration. When a case came to court, the local knowledge of grand and petty jurors was seen as an asset and helped to ensure that justice was done. If juries erred, it was usually on the side of leniency. As theft of goods worth one shilling or more was felony, and so a capital offence, juries repeatedly valued stolen goods at ten or eleven pence. Many of those condemned to death escaped the rope, often by reading a verse of the Bible and claiming benefit of clergy. Sentences of branding were rarely carried out. In a brutal age, the English penal code proved less brutal in practice than in theory.

Before depicting the law as just and mild reflection of a harmonious society, it is worth remarking that in the eighteenth century hundreds of new capital offences were created, most of them relating to property.

As customs duties on many goods were very high, smuggling became widespread, the nearest England came to organised crime. Public sympathy was usually with the smugglers: violent resistance was offered to customs officers and informers were beaten up or lynched. 'Smugglers Breaking Open the Kings Custom House at Poole, Oct. 7. 1747'. Dorset County Museum, Dorchester, Dorset

Practices which had once been tolerated were now forbidden. Increasingly rigorous game laws confined hunting rights to landowners. Gleaning and the keeping of odd scraps of material, once seen as workers' perquisites, were redefined as theft. This legislation could be seen as one facet of the growing social and cultural divide between the landed elite and the rest of society: some historians see it as evidence of a more general social polarisation. It is important, however, to distinguish between the making and enforcement of laws. While more and more capital offences were created, the number of executions fell. In Middlesex, under James I, an average of 150 people were executed each year: in 1750–70 the average was thirty and the same pattern is found elsewhere. Often the legislation was the product of a 'moral panic', of the type provoked by football hooliganism today. The Waltham Black Act of 1724 created some sixty new capital offences. It followed the appearance in Hampshire of large gangs of masked poachers, who had sinister links with Jacobitism. A late eighteenth-century legal writer noted:

> Laws of this kind commonly pass of course, without observation or debate. Having thus stolen into existence, they lie dormant on the statute book till they are notified to the world by the execution of some unthinking wretch who, to his utter astonishment, finds himself by law adjudged to die.

The concept of 'social crime', of crime as a form of quasi-political protest, is a modern one. Any credibility it has rests on the assertion that the State and the law are means through which the dominant elements in a society coerce and exploit the rest. Clearly, there were large areas to which this did not apply: the poor preyed upon each other more than they preyed upon the rich. Only by concentrating on socially discriminatory legislation, like the game laws, can the concept be made plausible. Moreover, those who talk of 'social crime' have to contend with the fact that many of the accused were acquitted or lightly punished: they are reduced to arguing that only by ostentatious shows of mercy and moderation could judges and JPs retain their credibility in the eyes of the lower orders. It is surely just as plausible that they were influenced by a sense of justice. JPs often showed bias, in favour of their friends, their tenants or their political party, but to suggest that they persistently misused their power for 'class' ends is as misguided as the assumption that the lower orders usually hated the rich. Eighteenth-century society had its tensions, but deference and paternalism remained strong. On some issues the different ranks in society had much in common. Local communities banded together against local rivals or outside interference, especially from central government and its revenue officers: smuggling was a national pastime.

CHAPTER SIX

POLITICS AND THE PEOPLE

We have already seen that popular interest in politics was considerable and that, in elections, 'the people' could choose between the persons and programmes of their superiors. But did the party divisions of the period have any real meaning? And could 'public opinion' have any real influence on the workings and policies of government?

The answer to the first question must be a resounding 'yes'. The conflicts between Whig and Tory bit deep into English life. They spilled from parliamentary into municipal elections. Charities and London hospitals had clear party biases. After political clubs emerged, in the Exclusion Crisis, many taverns and coffee-houses took on a definite party identity. Gangs from Whig and Tory 'mug-houses' did battle in London's streets, partisan crowds forced passers-by to drink the health of the hero of the hour—Monmouth in 1679, Sacheverell in 1710. Whigs and Tories read different newspapers, went to different race-meetings and were treated by different doctors. On election days, Whig and Tory mobs exchanged insults and blows. England might not be divided socially: it was undoubtedly divided politically.

What were the issues which aroused such strong emotions? One was religion: the Church of England was exceptionally militant in the generation after 1688 and hatred of Dissent was widespread. More generally, the Tory party came to express a general resentment of the changes wrought by the Revolution and of the strains of war—high taxes, the press-gang and a strange new order in which traditional standards of conduct seemed to have been forgotten: the Speaker of the Commons was expelled for bribery in 1695. Jumped-up financiers (often immigrants) made obscene profits in incomprehensible ways, while squires and their tenants struggled to pay the land-tax. Viscount Bolingbroke wrote, in 1709, that the previous twenty years had seen an inversion of the natural order; wealth had been transferred, through taxation, from the landed to the monied interest. The latter wielded great power, through institutions like the Bank, yet was accountable to no one. Unlike that of landowners, monied wealth was easily moved and conferred no social responsibilities. Last but not least, William III, George I and George II were foreigners and were accused of putting the interests of their Dutch or German homeland before those of England.

Toryism represented the conservative, Anglican, insular prejudices of provincial England, a cry of rage against civil servants and foreigners, financiers and Dissenters. It was anti-metropolitan and anti-cosmopolitan and drew great strength from traditional 'country' suspicion of London and of men in power. It was given a positive moral force by both Anglican religious conviction and an essentially religious view of monarchy. Belief in the divine right of kings may be alien to the secularly-minded twentieth century, but in the generations after the Revolution it proved very resilient. This showed the deep emotional roots of both religious views of monarchy and reverence for authority. Whereas modern writers presume (often on limited evidence) that their forebears must have resented authority, it is far from clear that most of them did so. Not all people are natural rebels: many crave order and authority and find reassurance in being told what to do. This was doubly true in an age when educational opportunities were limited, when most people saw little prospect of improving the lot to which they had been born and when the Church depicted obedience to authority as a religious obligation. In such a society 'obedience or subjection becomes so familiar that most men never make any enquiry about its origin or cause, more than about the principle of gravity.'

As we have seen, the Revolution did not destroy belief in divine-right monarchy: suppressed under William, it re-emerged stronger than ever under Anne. By now, however, it was clear that she would be the last Protestant Stuart. When she died, Tories would have to choose between a Catholic Stuart and a German Lutheran. Many hoped the Pretender would resolve this dilemma by becoming a Protestant, but he refused. So George I became king and, despite the rebellions of 1715 and 1745, the Hanoverian dynasty survived. The strength of Jacobitism remains a matter for conjecture. Active conspirators were probably relatively few, but many more viewed the Hanoverian regime with distaste and hoped that a Stuart king might be better. Under William some Whigs, often radical Whigs, had argued that James, restored on strict conditions, would abuse his powers less than William. If such Whig Jacobitism had disappeared by 1714, many simple people (with no personal knowledge of the doltish, bibulous Pretender) saw him as an idealised 'just prince' — rather as many country people had seen Monmouth as the 'true king' in 1685. At times it seems that crowds chanted Jacobite slogans simply because they were likely to prove especially offensive to those in authority. Clearly, those expressing Jacobite sympathies were far more numerous than those ready to take Jacobite action. Many drank healths to 'the king over the water', but it was alleged that 'no people in the universe know better the difference between drinking and fighting'. Nevertheless, it is clear that Whig ministers took the Jacobite threat very seriously and that Jacobite emotions remained strong among rich and poor, in town and country. Their persistence helps to explain the resilience of Toryism during the long Whig ascendancy after 1714.

Jacobite sympathies remained strong long after an active Jacobite movement ended. Large numbers of Jacobite glasses survive; this one, showing the Old Pretender, dates from about fifteen years after Culloden. Phillips Fine Art Auctioneers

By contrast the Whigs' appeal was less to emotion than to interest. It was vital for liberty and property, they argued, that James (or his son) should not return. The national interest made it necessary to continue the war on the continent, even if it seemed mainly for the benefit of England's allies. Even toleration for Dissent was justified partly in prudential terms: persecution was bad for business. Only when exploiting anti-Popery did the Whigs match the Tory appeal to gut emotion. Where the Whigs really scored was in political and administrative expertise. Under William there emerged a new breed of Whigs, who did not share the Exclusionists' suspicion of power. These 'Junto' Whigs wanted power: they piloted financial legislation through Parliament, built up the new system of government credit and organised the war. While the Tory leaders bickered, the Junto pulled together and pressed William and Anne to follow their advice. After 1714, they denounced the Tories as Jacobites and wrung from the complaisant George I a monopoly of power.

That monopoly depended on their establishing a solid Whig majority in the Commons and so on their ability to win elections. Under William and Anne these were more frequent than at any time before or since. Under the Triennial Act of 1694 no more than three years could elapse between elections: in fact there were ten between 1695 and 1715. As there were several bitterly divisive issues at this time—the succession, the wars, the Church—these elections were vigorously contested and their outcome closely followed shifts in public opinion. Thus in 1708 the Whigs won, following an abortive Jacobite rising in Scotland. Two years later, war-weariness and the Sacheverell trial helped to bring about a crushing Tory victory. Peace with France brought an even bigger Tory landslide in 1713. It has been calculated that more than four per cent of the population (or nearly twenty per cent of adult males) had the vote under Anne: much the same percentage as in the years *after* the 1832 Reform Bill.

If Parliament ever, before the days of mass democracy, represented the 'national will', it did so under Anne. Moreover, of the two parties, the Tories were the stronger: 1708 was the only clear Whig victory of the reign. The Whigs might be clever and 'progressive': they were not popular. When, in 1715, the Whigs again won a majority, they set out to ensure that the electors would not come up with the wrong answer again. The Septennial Act of 1716 increased the maximum interval between elections from three years to seven. Meanwhile George's Whig ministers extracted every iota of electoral advantage from the Crown's much enlarged patronage. William and Anne had refused to allow either party full control of their patronage: if either became too strong in Parliament, its leaders would try to impose their will on the monarch. Now the Tories were damned in George's eyes by the '15: the Whigs had their chance. Every government office, no matter how minor, every dignity in the

Church, every military commission was used to advance Whig electoral interests. Great Whig landowners, like the Dukes of Bedford and Devonshire, spent heavily building up an 'interest' in small boroughs. They built town halls and assembly rooms, found jobs for the kinsmen of aldermen, gave lavishly to local charities and patronised local tradesmen. Together, careful management of the 'government interest' and heavy spending by Whig magnates gave the Whigs control of enough small boroughs to ensure a constant majority in the Commons. The Union with Scotland added another 45 docile Scots Whig MPs to the Westminster Parliament.

Such methods did not make elections a total sham. The system had always been open to manipulation. Gentlemen marched their tenants to the polls and watched them vote: poll books show whole villages following their landlord's lead. The family in the 'big house' always wielded great influence in a one-horse town. In the past, however, such influence had never been systematically exploited, either by the Crown or by a party. Now it was. Where possible the Whigs reduced the electorate. In many boroughs contests had been rare and there were differing opinions as to the extent of the franchise. Candidates naturally espoused the one which gave them the best chance. The Tories under Anne, conscious of their popularity, usually plumped for the broader one. The Whigs, under George I and II, preferred a narrow one, so that government officials and the recipients of Whig or government largesse would make up a large part of the electorate. Such methods did not always work. Shire electorates were far too big to be bribed or browbeaten; often Tory landowners also greatly outnumbered Whigs. Even very small electorates could swallow the candidates' beer, beef and money and then vote the other way. But they worked often enough for the Whigs to sustain their majority from 1715 to the 1750s.

This did not make Parliament wholly unrepresentative. There was always a substantial minority of Tory MPs, often representing counties and the larger boroughs. It was a testimony to the strength of Tory principles that the Tories' local organisation remained so vigorous despite forty years in the political wilderness. Besides, Whig MPs did not slavishly do as ministers bade them. Although Walpole and his successors (Henry Pelham and his brother, the Duke of Newcastle) were accused of buying the Commons' support with places and pensions, the placemen and pensioners were outnumbered by independent Whig backbenchers; these were keen to maintain the electors' goodwill, especially in the run-up to

---

(Pages 77–8) *Votes were recorded in poll books, which often show whole villages voting the same way, as the squire directed. This one, from Norfolk, records a poll of 1734.* Norfolk County Library

A

COPY of the POLL

FOR THE

Knights of the Shire

For the COUNTY of

NORFOLK,

Taken at NORWICH, *May* 22. 1734.

CANDIDATES:

Sir EDMUND BACON, *Bar*.
WILLIAM WODEHOUSE, *Efq*;
The Honourable ROBERT COKE.
WILLIAM MORDEN, *Efq*;

Printed in the Year MDCCXXXIV.

Residences.	Freeholds.	B.	W.	C.	M.
Moon Christopher	Hickling				
Perkins Valentine					
Plumstead Edmund					
Steel James					
Wells John					
Wells Robert					
Colton Fore. H.		10	7	2	4
Briggs Clement	Honningham				
Brown John, *Esq*;					
Daveney Henry					
Parlam Thomas					
Vincent Richard					
Congham Freb. L.		3	3	2	2
Pigg Thomas	G. Massingham				
Corpusty S. Erp. H.		0	0	1	1
Money Stephen	Briston				
Costesy Fore. H.		1	1	0	0
Gunton Benjamin					
Coston Fore. H.		1	1	0	0
Riches John					
Coulston al. Colveston Grim. H.		1	1	0	0
Glascock Thomas	Hockd. & Wil.				
Cranworth Mitt. H.		0	0	1	1
Howell William	Neckton				
Hudson John					
Saltier Nathaniel, *Clerk.*					
		3	2	0	0

an election. Opposition from backbench Whigs and a vocal public opinion led Walpole to drop his plans for a general excise in 1733 and Pelham to repeal the much misrepresented Jewish Naturalisation Bill in 1753.

Under William and Anne politics was volatile and dramatic. The Commons' composition changed frequently; MPs were often truculent, not least because the strains of war created new issues and animosities. In these unpropitious circumstances, monarchs and ministers had to extract large sums of money from Parliament. With elections so frequent, politicians were especially sensitive to the public mood outside Westminster. In 1701–2 popular pressure helped persuade William's Tory ministers of the need for war with France; in 1710 clear signs of popular hostility to the Whigs and their war led Anne to dismiss her Whig ministers and call an election. Under George I things quietened down. Money bills sailed through the Commons, backbenchers no longer asked to see the government's accounts. Walpole's critics cried that he had sapped Parliament's, and the nation's, moral fibre, that money ruled all. In fact his political machine worked so smoothly because he carefully avoided measures which would antagonise Whig backbenchers or Whig electors. The limitations imposed by (Whig) public opinion were not obvious because he imposed them on himself, rather than wait for others to impose them upon him: but that made them no less real. Occasionally he misjudged the mood—over the excise in 1733, over war with Spain in 1739—and then he backed down. The potential for a more effective system of representation had been anaesthetised, not killed. With the collapse of the old party system in the 1750s and the re-emergence of divisive issues in the 1760s, one-party rule was no longer possible. The electoral process regained much of its meaning and some began to agitate for electoral reform.

It would be misleading, however, to see the political world of the first two Georges as wholly serene. Election results might be monotonously consistent, but each time there was the hope (or fear) of change and many were vigorously contested. Candidates might have little respect for electors—one regretted the need for 'infamous and disreputable compliance with the low habits of venal wretches'—but they still had to pander to their greed and whims. Candidates' wives gritted their teeth as farmers tramped through their homes in hobnailed boots, duchesses kissed greasy tradesmen, gentlemen forced down inedible food and patiently bore affronts which normally they would have repaid with blows. Bribery was rife, lavish expenditure on food and drink was expected as of right. With drink, insults flew, tempers frayed and blows were exchanged.

This is not to suggest that elections were simply an excuse to get drunk, fight and pocket the candidates' money. A French visitor remarked in 1747, 'In this country the children in all conditions of life suck in party with their mother's milk.' Partisan interest was sustained by the press. Few successful politicians can have been vilified so consistently and so violently, in print and pamphlet, as Walpole. While historians stress the placidity of Parliamentary politics, foreigners were struck by the boldness with which Londoners (especially) criticised the government. There, more than in being able to influence what that government did, lay the essence of the 'freeborn Englishman'. 'The equality of English privileges' wrote Dr Johnson, 'the impartiality of our laws, the freedom of our tenures and the prosperity of our trade dispose us very little to reverence of superiors.' ('Rule Britannia', with its refrain, 'Britons never never never shall be slaves', dates from the 1740s). There was an element of bombast and self-delusion about this attitude, as there was in eulogies of the 'roast beef of old England', which many could not afford, and vocal contempt for the downtrodden French. But there was a certain reality behind the bombast. Watermen and porters barged gentlemen out of their way. The street was the 'mob's' territory: a lady whose coach blocked a right of way found people using it as a thoroughfare. The elite seems to have taken this insubordination in good part and to have responded in kind: gentlemen who were jostled in the street sought satisfaction with their fists.

The 'insolence' of the 'meaner sort' towards their 'betters' often shocked foreigners. It was most marked in London, whose citizens (like New Yorkers today) seem almost to have taken pride in the dangers of living in the capital. Rural communities seem to have been more deferential although plebeian truculence was by no means confined to London. But what, one might ask, did it achieve (other than the satisfaction of cocking a snook at authority)? Clearly it found expression in elections, but they were infrequent and, while the popular will sometimes dictated the results, more were determined by money and influence, without the inconvenience of a contest. There were other forms of action—petitions, addresses from electors, lobbying and riot. This last was a common form of popular action and, thanks to the weakness of the State's police resources, it was often effective. As we have seen with reference to 1688, riots had their own rules or conventions. Rioters aimed to frighten, hurt or humiliate their victims or to destroy their property: fatalities (and outright theft) were rare. The corollary of the belief that the law gave rights to 'freeborn Englishmen' was a strong sense of legality. Riots were rarely mindless and undirected. Most defended certain norms of behaviour: rioters believed that they had right on their side and that it was the law that they were taking into their own hands. Often they rioted only after appealing in vain to the proper authorities—to have grain brought to the market, to defend age-old common rights against encroachment. Most were defensive: if they had a political content, it was a call for the preservation of 'ancient English liberties'. The rights which they defended might not

David Hume, a Scottish writer with a decided bias towards anglicisation. To him England was a model to be followed. Oil painting by Allan Ramsay. The poet Robert Burns *(overleaf)* had a very different view about Scotland's relationship with England. To him the Union with England had destroyed much of what was distinctively Scottish. Oil painting by Nasmyth. *Scottish National Portrait Gallery*

always be recognised by those in authority. Poaching gangs harked back to the days before the game laws; smugglers gained so much support because many thought heavy import duties were unfair; the press-gang was hated as an infringement of individual liberty; but that did not make riots into social protests. Gentlemen enjoyed their contraband brandy and protected their labourers against the recruiting officer: the government, rather than the gentry, was normally seen as the enemy.

The political content of riots under the first two Georges does not suggest that 'the people' had developed ideas or objectives markedly different from those of their superiors. From the 1750s this began to change.

When John Wilkes emerged as a popular hero in the 1760s, manufacturers were quick to exploit his popularity. This rare wine glass is engraved with a bird perched on top of an open cage flanked by flowers, and below the inscription 'LIBERTY AND WILKES'. Phillips Fine Art Auctioneers

81

Stock phrases about 'English liberties', 'freedom' and 'Revolution principles' were given a more radical twist by the likes of Wilkes and Paine. They came to be understood (by some) not as the liberties men now possessed under the law, but as those they ought to have in a fairer, more equal society. Until that time, 'the people' debated, petitioned and took sides on issues which preoccupied the aristocracy, but did not challenge the aristocracy's right to rule, or put forward demands of their own. Thus while the aristocracy took the people's interventions seriously, they posed no real threat to its political hegemony. Such a consensus about the social basis of politics was not to last for long. By the end of the century some demanded radical changes, even democracy. In such a changed world Walpole's methods of electoral management would prove both ineffectual and obnoxious. At first, the elite responded to calls for reform with repression which, in the backlash provoked by the French Revolution, won much public support. Yet, slowly, change came. The rich forest of government patronage was gradually thinned and, in the nineteenth century, successive reform acts dismantled the old electoral system.

This could not have been predicted in 1688 and would not have been welcomed by most of those who made the Revolution. They had wished to preserve the aristocracy's control of politics against the threat of absolutism. If few relished the licensed misrule and rough and tumble of the electoral process, they appreciated its value in protecting the Commons against royal attempts at manipulation. One reason why the elite was so attached to Parliament may be that they were confident of their ability to control it, because they shared many of the beliefs and values of the electorate. Often, indeed, threats to aristocratic power and privilege had come more from the Crown than the lower orders. It would seem, then, that there was much continuity in electoral politics between the reigns of Charles II and George II: that, indeed, was what the Revolution had been intended to achieve. Yet this same electoral system, however imperfect and open to abuse it might be, was capable of adapting to changing circumstances. Elite control over the electorate was always precarious and depended on there remaining a basic agreement on the fundamentals of the constitution. Once that agreement began to crumble, England's representative system allowed for the deployment of peaceful pressure for change, while in general England's aristocracy proved more pragmatic and pliant than most in the face of demands for change. In the words of that great political fixer, the Duke of Newcastle, 'If we go on despising what people think or say, we shall not have it long in our power to direct what measures shall be taken.' If ministers thought that way even in the serene 1740s, they were to pay far more heed to the people's wishes in the following century.

CHAPTER SEVEN

BRITAIN AND THE WORLD

Before 1688 England was not a major European power. In the sixteenth and seventeenth centuries continental kingdoms, like France and Spain, became more centralised and developed large bureaucracies and standing armies, mainly because they needed to mobilise resources more efficiently for war. England's government remained much as it had been in the late Middle Ages, decentralised and amateurish. The sea allowed English monarchs to opt out of European power-politics, frequent misunderstandings between kings and Parliaments meant that they did not have the money to opt in. This relative isolation did not, however, prevent the English from extending their horizons. Their trade became more extensive and was backed up by a powerful navy. Successive Navigation Acts sought to exclude the Dutch and other foreign powers from the increasingly lucrative trade with England's colonies. Under Louis XIV France emerged as a serious commercial and colonial competitor, not least because the French wished to settle in those areas in which England was most interested—North America and the Caribbean. European political rivalries extended worldwide and colonial and commercial conflicts had important repercussions in Europe.

The Revolution forced England to become enmeshed in European affairs. To prevent James's restoration, England had to join wholeheartedly in a massive war. Peace came in 1697 but four years later Louis reopened the succession issue by recognising James's son as James III, on his father's death. This led to another great war, from 1702–13, in which geopolitical and commercial questions also bulked large. In 1700 the last Habsburg king of Spain died and bequeathed his throne to Louis' grandson. This threatened to bring together the territories of France and Spain, in Europe and the New World, in an empire whose resources and military power would dwarf those of other European states. Meanwhile, English traders feared that the French would prove far more formidable competitors than the Spaniards, especially in the Mediterranean and Latin America. Increasingly, then, dynastic, diplomatic and economic interests were combining to draw England into European affairs. The energy with which England's government mobilised resources for war and the success of English armies and fleets established England as a major power which could not (and did not wish to) be left out on the periphery in future. In the eighteenth century, England fought in more and bigger wars than ever before, enhancing her European standing and extending her trade and empire.

In material terms this international success proved a mixed blessing. On one hand, the colonial trades brought prosperity to many, especially in London and the west coast ports—Bristol, Liverpool, Whitehaven and Glasgow. England imported sugar and tobacco from the New World and spices and textiles from the east: many of these goods were re-exported to Europe. The growth of the North American colonies created a major market for English manufacturers—Birmingham metal wares, West Riding woollens. Habits changed, the quality of life was enriched. Tea and coffee became everyday beverages, despite complaints that tea addled the mind and that coffee-houses were haunts of faction and sedition. Styles and designs became more cosmopolitan: Chinese porcelain was imported in large quantities, furniture was decorated with Chinese lacquer. Trade and travel also brought influences from nearer home. Queen Mary helped to create a fashion for blue Delft ware, young men on the 'Grand Tour' developed a taste for classical antiquity. French fashions, for clothes and furniture, headgear and gardens, were widely imitated. Such a diversification of styles and tastes was not confined to the elite. Greater prosperity created a wider market which manufacturers were quick to exploit. Thanks to pattern-books, Chippendale chairs and Adam fireplaces or muffin-dishes could be found in quite modest homes. Josiah Wedgwood was one of the first to combine mass-production with quality and taste. Skilful marketing encouraged people to buy articles, not because they needed them, but because they were fashionable.

Thus colonial and commercial expansion brought more foreign goods and influences to England; but who benefited? The upper and middle ranks of society could, of course, afford these new goods and fashions, but so could many of the less well off. As production of colonial commodities increased, prices fell: tea, coffee, sugar and tobacco were no longer luxuries. Mass-production began to bring down the price of consumer goods. Yet there was a price to pay—above all, higher taxes. As we have seen, the old principle that the poorest should be exempt was abandoned in 1688: it was argued that, as they received the benefits of government, they should pay for them. The poor were also most at risk from the recruiting sergeant and the press-gang: having no economically useful skills, they would find it hard to secure protection from landlord or employer. As so often, the Revolution benefited the rich and middling sort—but not the poor.

While China produced goods for the British market, English manufacturers copied Chinese styles, as in this rare Worcester vase, painted in the rich Kakiemon style, c. 1765. Phillips Fine Art Auctioneers

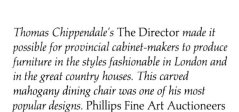

Thomas Chippendale's The Director *made it possible for provincial cabinet-makers to produce furniture in the styles fashionable in London and in the great country houses. This carved mahogany dining chair was one of his most popular designs.* Phillips Fine Art Auctioneers

Hogarth's 'The Gate of Calais (or the Roast Beef of Old England)' was inspired by his arrest at Calais as a suspected spy. It captures beautifully English contempt for foreigners, especially the French. The Mansell Collection

If the growth of trade and empire did much to improve the Englishman's quality of life, it is less certain that it broadened his mind. A few intellectuals were deeply impressed by the moral qualities of the civilisations of the New World. This led some to query the story of the Fall or to ask how Christianity could claim to be the only true religion. Others used an idealised 'noble savage' to highlight the decadence of their own society. For most, however, military and commercial success reinforced a national pride, or arrogance, to which they were already all too prone and to which the words of 'Rule Britannia' bear ample testimony. They saw the French as sly and spineless, ready to cheat English visitors, but under the thumb of the soldiery and the priests. Foreigners were generally seen as stupid, servile and in every way inferior to the English: if they had the temerity to visit England they risked being insulted, even assaulted, in the streets.

Such insularity was not simply the result of ignorance. English readers were well informed about foreign wars and international relations: newspapers carried a great deal of foreign news, which was politically 'safer' than domestic. More English people travelled abroad in the eighteenth century than ever before. Young aristocrats, fresh from the rigours of public school, were packed off on the 'Grand Tour' with a tutor, who had the thankless task of instilling a little culture into his charge and keeping him out of the taverns and brothels. Tens of thousands of soldiers and sailors were given the chance, often against their will, to visit foreign parts. In some cases, doubtless, travel did indeed broaden the mind. Some bought classical statues and old masters (many of them genuine), others developed a taste for the civilised lifestyle of Italy: even hardline Protestants were courteously received at Rome by urbane cardinals. More often, however, travel served (then as now) only to heighten awareness of the differences between life at home and life abroad and to reinforce the belief that the former was infinitely preferable.

Nevertheless, English attitudes towards foreigners were not unremittingly hostile. The English might insult passing Frenchmen in the streets, but they imitated French fashions. Foreigners found the English cold, morose and quarrelsome, hard-working and obsessed with gambling. They drank heavily without becoming cheerful and continentals found the English Sunday a penance. However, those who tried to get to know the English, and who got away from London and the major tourist centres, found them more welcoming, if still somewhat reserved. The complexity of English attitudes was seen also in their treatment of immigrants. In the sixteenth and seventeenth centuries thousands of Protestants fled to England to escape religious persecution, first from the Low Countries ('Walloons') and then from France ('Huguenots'). Most had easily transportable skills—craftsmen, sailors, business people. (Farmers who relied on their knowledge of local soils and climate were far less inclined to move.) Most settled near the south and east coasts, at Norwich and Colchester, Canterbury and Southampton and above all in London. Their expertise helped the English woollen industry to begin to catch up with the more advanced manufactures of Flanders. Some traded, using their contacts with friends and kin who had stayed behind. Many prospered: at least ten per cent of the first subscriptions to the Bank of England came from Huguenots, who also provided the first governor, Sir John Houblon.

In many ways the Huguenots were made welcome. The English felt considerable solidarity with oppressed Protestants on the continent. They were hard-working and looked after their own poor; but jealousies sometimes arose. Some were due to misunderstandings: they were mistaken for Catholics or caught up in a general suspicion of foreigners, like that which swept London in the weeks after the Great Fire. More often, they were seen as too successful and as threatening the livelihoods of Englishmen. In 1675 London silkweavers rioted in protest against new power-looms, which (it was said) would throw thousands out of work. Huguenots' houses were attacked, looms were smashed and at least one person was killed. Violence on such a scale was rare, but many Huguenots and their

The appointment of a merchant of Huguenot descent, Sir John Houblon, as first Governor of the Bank of England, was a fitting illustration of the Huguenots' contribution both to English trade and finance and to the war effort against France. By courtesy of the Governor and Company of the Bank of England

Like many later groups of immigrants, Huguenots who came to London settled in poorer districts, especially the East End. Some visible signs of their presence remain in Spitalfields in (above) *this terrace in Fournier Street, and* (below) *a former Huguenot church which later became a synagogue and is now a mosque.* Greater London Photograph Library

property were subjected to petty insults and assaults. Town councils subjected them to tighter regulations than native craftsmen. Small wonder that they huddled together in distinct communities, like that in Spitalfields, East London, which still bears marks of its Huguenot past.

In the 1680s, as persecution intensified in France, a new wave of Huguenot immigrants arrived. This time the public, moved by stories of the cruelties they had undergone, received them more sympathetically, although one MP urged the Commons in 1693 to kick 'these Frogs' out of the kingdom. The House ordered that the speech be burned, but would not agree to naturalise the Huguenots and so allow them to trade on equal terms. During the French wars, however, Huguenots brought both first-hand knowledge and a fierce commitment to the war effort. As the flood of immigrants slowed to a trickle and as a second and a third generation grew up, English-speaking and attuned to the English ways, the Huguenots became increasingly integrated into English society. An actor of Huguenot descent, David Garrick, became perhaps the greatest interpreter of Shakespeare in the eighteenth century.

Other immigrants were less fortunate. An attempt by Whig ministers in 1709 to encourage Protestant refugees from the Palatinate to come to England was bitterly attacked by Tories as a threat to the jobs (and probably the wives) of English workers. The Irish, of course, were disliked both as Papists and as Irish. The Jews were perhaps most vulnerable of all. They were first officially allowed to settle in the 1650s—another instance where Cromwell's tolerance was far in advance of his time—but their legal position remained precarious and they survived on sufferance. Some, mostly from Spain and Portugal, were comparatively westernised and became integrated, as far as they could, into English society. Others, from Eastern Europe, kept themselves aloof and rigorously preserved their separate identity. A group of those who were most keen to assimilate, led by the banker Sir Samson Gideon, in 1753 promoted a bill which would have allowed Jews to apply for naturalisation without conforming to the Church of England. It provoked a hysterical outcry. Henry Pelham, taken aback, hastily had the bill repealed. The Jewish community returned to the twilight zone after some very unpleasant months in the limelight.

The Jews were unusually unfortunate. Despite the robust chauvinism of the English, immigrants did settle and assimilate in the eighteenth century. With the eclipse of the Tory party, the government became more sympathetic. Like Prussia and the Dutch Republic, most Whigs believed that immigrants should be encouraged for the skills they brought: it did not matter to them, as it did to the Tories, that they were not Anglicans. The long Whig ascendancy after 1714, indeed, saw a cooling of religious conflict: zeal and bigotry became unfashionable. Was this yet another consequence of the Revolution?

CHAPTER EIGHT

RELIGION

The Revolution produced one major piece of religious legislation. The Toleration Act of 1689 allowed Protestant nonconformists to worship in their own meeting-houses, provided these had been licensed by a JP. In retrospect this was seen as guaranteeing individual liberty in the spiritual sphere, just as the Bill of Rights was said to have done in the temporal. It ended religious persecution in England (at least as far as Protestants were concerned) and probably helped to foster a spirit of tolerance which was to make it easier for immigrants to settle. These were developments which liberal, humane people in later generations could not but applaud. However, the Act was passed in a spirit far removed from liberalism and humanity, was widely seen as a disaster and led to a generation and more of bitter religious strife.

Until the civil war, few doubted that the Church of England should embrace the whole community. People might disagree about the form the Church should take, but all agreed that it should be uniform. In the 1640s, however, some put forward a new view of a 'church', as a select, exclusive group of true believers. Trusting wholly in God, they did not presume to impose upon others their view of divine truth. For the first time, there emerged a belief that church membership should be voluntary, that compulsion in religion was wrong and that religious pluralism was permissible. Not all the sects shared these views: some claimed that, as the Lord's chosen people, they should impose their beliefs on others. Nevertheless by 1660 it was clear that a small but determined minority would never willingly belong to any national church.

The Church of England was restored at the Restoration, much as it had been before the civil wars. The initiative for this came from the Anglican laity and clergy. They saw the destruction of the old church in the 1640s as having unleashed insubordination and confusion, exemplified by the Quakers, with their refusal to doff their hats or use other marks of respect towards superiors. The old church, hierarchical in structure, with power flowing down from above, seemed an essential prop of the old hierarchical social and political order, which had so recently been overturned. But the motives for restoring the church were not only political.

Attempts to root out Anglican practices and festivals had shown how strongly entrenched these were. Parishioners forcibly resisted the expulsion of Anglican parsons in the 1640s and equally forcibly reinstated them at the Restoration. Many had theological objections to, say, adult baptism or the Quakers' rejection of Biblical authority in favour of the 'inner light'. Some wished to enjoy some revenge for persecution suffered under Puritan rule. Last but not least, to many the ideal of a single national church remained valid. They believed that truth was indivisible, and so was not a subject for compromise, and that a single church was necessary for a united society. Moreover, only a church to which all had to belong could maintain effective discipline over its members. People were not naturally good; churches taught them what was right and wrong and punished them if they sinned: fornicators stood before the congregation in a white sheet, as an example to others. The restoration of the Church, then, implied an intention to reassert the Church's moral and spiritual role in society.

Along with the Church's restoration went a barrage of new laws against Protestant nonconformity, which have often been denounced as a retrograde step by Nonconformist historians and by those writing in more tolerant times. It seems unlikely, however, that more than a small (if vocal) minority actively disapproved of this legislation. A religious census of 1676 suggested that Dissenters made up about four per cent of the population; although this was an under-estimate, it helps to put the problem of nonconformity into perspective. Not all members of the Church of England were hostile to Dissent, however. Some who conformed at the Restoration were influenced by the Puritan tradition within the Church and had much sympathy with those of similar views who had refused to conform. Others, the Latitudinarians, argued that the differences between Anglican and Dissenter mattered less than the many things which united them. Reacting against the enthusiasm of the civil war years, they urged peace and tolerance: the basic truths were few and simple, God was kind and merciful. While more rigid 'High Church' Anglicans, and the Dissenters, argued from positions of entrenched certainty, Latitudinarians advocated a cooler, blander approach, in which persecution had no part.

In Charles II's reign, it seems likely that the High Church clergy were the strongest element: they were certainly the most vocal, supporting James and the Tory party vigorously during and after the Exclusion Crisis. The old Puritans and Latitudinarians inclined towards the Whigs, who for reasons of both principle and expediency sought to relax the laws against Dissent. Most Whigs were hostile neither to revealed religion nor to Anglican theology: what they resented was 'priestcraft'—the clergy's determination to impose their will on the laity. Hostility to 'priestcraft' stemmed partly from the English tradition of anticlericalism—the clergy should be kept firmly subordinated to the laity—and partly from the newer belief that religion was a matter for individual choice and individual conscience. Persecution was thus morally wrong, discouraged immigrants and harassed useful citizens. Besides, as Dissenters mostly lived in towns, they made up a disproportionately large part of the electorate and the Whigs wanted their votes.

The Whigs' defeat in the Exclusion Crisis was followed by a vigorous persecution of Dissent. Then, to the Tories' amazement, James turned against them and courted the Dissenters. Alarmed, the Church's leaders put in a counter-bid for their support, appealing to a sense of Protestant solidarity against Popery and offering both 'comprehension' and 'toleration'. Changes would be made in the liturgy to accommodate those Dissenters whose only objection to the Church was that it retained ceremonies which they disliked. For those who wanted no part of an established church, they matched James's offer of liberty of worship. It worked: leading Dissenters visited the Seven Bishops in the Tower, amid much talk of reconciliation. By a supreme irony, James's advocacy of toleration seemed set to secure it for everyone except those for whom he most wanted it—the Catholics.

William's invasion changed matters drastically. A Calvinist himself, he was cool towards the High Church bishops and their lay allies, while welcoming approaches from Dissenters. Churchmen thus came to see William not only as a usurper but as an enemy to the Church. Their earlier enthusiasm for changes in the liturgy evaporated: Archbishop Sancroft said that he was still ready to discuss the matter, but 'he believed the Dissenters would never agree among themselves with what concessions they would be satisfied.' Some Dissenters, indeed, appealed directly to William to settle 'the terms of the union wherein all the reformed churches agree', which raised the fear that he might even impose comprehension, without consulting the bishops. However fearful and resentful the Churchmen might be, they could not wholly renegue on their offers of the previous year. Bills for comprehension and toleration were introduced in Parliament. After much behind-the-scenes negotiation, it was agreed (in effect) to drop the former in return for the latter's being allowed to pass.

The Toleration Act reached the statute book thanks to a sordid backstage deal and represented the very least the Churchmen could do to fulfil their promises. While it gave most Dissenters virtually complete religious liberty, it was intended that their political disabilities should remain. The Test and Corporation Acts, requiring office-holders to take communion in an Anglican church, remained in force until 1828. Even so, for those who believed there should be close bond between Church and State, the Act was a severe blow. Dissent flourished, while Anglican con-

gregations dwindled. The weakening of clerical authority and the lapsing of censorship made possible the publication of works attacking the very foundations of revealed religion. What was worse, similar views were advanced by maverick Anglicans: Benjamin Hoadly, who denied the need for churches, or a liturgy, ended his days as Bishop of Winchester. Anxious Churchmen linked these challenges to the Church's authority and Christian orthodoxy with what many saw as a collapse of public morals: corruption in public life, dubious financial dealings in the City, crime in the streets and 'lewdness' in the theatre.

Faced with the prospect of subsiding into the bottomless pit, the High Church clergy fought back. They could expect little leadership from the bishops. Sancroft and six of his colleagues had quit rather than swear allegiance to William and Mary and their replacements were Latitudinarians and wimpish moderates, with no sympathy for High Church views. So the clergy and their lay allies betook themselves to politics, taking as their text 'the church in danger'. They concentrated their fire on two 'loopholes' in the Toleration Act—the failure to prohibit Dissenting schools and the practice of occasional conformity. Many Dissenters evaded the intention of the law and qualified for office by taking Anglican communion once a year, while attending meeting-houses at other times. To High Churchmen, this profaned the sacrament and their hostility was so strong that in 1704 the Tory majority in the Commons put the war effort at risk in their eagerness to force through a bill against it. Under Anne, indeed, militant High Churchmen preached sermons on the sort of texts which had once been the speciality of extreme Puritans, such as 'Break their tongues, O God, in their mouths'. And of all these fiery parsons, the most militant of all was Henry Sacheverell.

Any view of the Revolution as a triumph of liberalism and moderation, welcomed by the English people, cannot easily accommodate Dr Sacheverell. In 1710 the Commons impeached him for seditious libel, following a splenetic sermon in which he berated not only the Whig ministers but the Revolution. Insofar as his meaning could be understood, he had allegedly argued that resistance, 'the necessary means used to bring about the said happy Revolution' was 'odious and unjustifiable'; he had described the Toleration Act as 'unreasonable' and 'unwarrantable' and in attacking the ministry, he had allegedly defamed the Queen, who had appointed

---

Contrasting Dissenting chapels: (Above) *Keach's meeting house at Winslow, Buckinghamshire, c. 1695, a small nondescript building for a plebeian rural congregation.* Royal Commission on the Historical Monuments of England
(Below) *The Octagon Chapel, Norwich, c. 1760, built for an affluent urban congregation. The large windows show that there was now little danger of their being smashed by Anglican mobs. Pencil and grey wash by James Sillett, 1764–1840.* Norfolk Museums Service (Norwich Castle Museum)

it. The Commons failed to make good their case and the Lords let Sacheverell off with a nominal sentence. While the trial was going on, large crowds demolished and burned meeting-houses, stoned the homes of leading Whigs and were stopped by troops on their way to attack the Bank. Afterwards Sacheverell was fêted in every town he visited and the reaction caused by his trial helped to sweep the Tories to power in the 1710 general election. Soon after, Acts were passed against occasional conformity and Dissenting schools.

The Toleration Act, it would seem, was the product of a peculiar set of circumstances and did not reflect the views of the majority. That it survived and toleration eventually became accepted owed less to its merits than to the Whig ascendancy after 1714. High Church views were far from dead, but they could not now find effective expression. The Tory minority in the Commons could not influence ecclesiastical policy, the clergy's representative assembly (Convocation) ceased to function and High Churchmen were excluded from preferment (while Hoadly was promoted again and again). Walpole, preferring to avoid controversy, largely left the Churchmen alone, but Parliament passed some vindictively anticlerical measures in the 1730s. For many Whig politicians, the Church was useful mainly as a source of patronage: bishops were appointed on political grounds and their first responsibility was to attend the Lords regularly. Many, in fact, performed their ecclesiastical tasks conscientiously, but they were not dynamic leaders, nor did they challenge their political masters' views on religion.

Shorn of its coercive powers, the Church had to learn to compete if it was to survive. In many parishes church attendance declined and it found it hard to meet the challenge posed by new industrial communities (not least because an Act of Parliament was needed to create a new parish). Elsewhere, it fared better. In many rural parishes, squires like the fictional Sir Roger de Coverley ensured that villagers trooped obediently to church to 'hear their duties explained to them and join together in adoration of the Supreme Being'. In small city-centre parishes in London, Norwich and elsewhere an informed and committed Tory laity provided strong support for the parson. There were attempts to improve the pay of the poorer clergy (Queen Anne's Bounty) and a commission was set up to build fifty new churches in and around London. They were certainly needed: the parish of Stepney contained 75,000 people—more than any provincial town; it now gained three new churches. In the end, only twelve were built, partly because they were constructed on a lavish scale, but this at least ensured that London's suburbs were better provided with churches than the new industrial towns.

A different type of Anglican initiative came in the religious societies (essentially social and spiritual), organisations to bring religion to the poor

William and Mary did much to popularise Delft ware, often bearing their portraits. Lambeth Delft plate portraying William and Mary. *Museum of London*

Josiah Wedgwood was a pioneer in the mass production of quality goods, making available classical elegance at a modest price. Snake-handled or 'Venus' vase depicting Venus in her chariot drawn by swans, inspired by a painting by Vigee le Burn, *c.*1785. *Courtesy of the Trustees of the Wedgwood Museum, Barlaston, Staffordshire*

Under James II, the Earl of Tyrconnell set out to overthrow the English Protestant domination of Ireland, only to be thwarted by the Revolution. Painting by an artist of the French School, *c.* 1690. *By courtesy of the National Portrait Gallery, London*

While the City of London had a superabundance of parish churches (more than a hundred), the population of many suburban parishes grew to a point where the churches could no longer accommodate more than a tiny fraction of the people. New churches like St George in the East (above), Christ Church, Spitalfields (below left), and St Anne's, Stepney (below right), represented an attempt to cope with this problem. Greater London Photograph Library

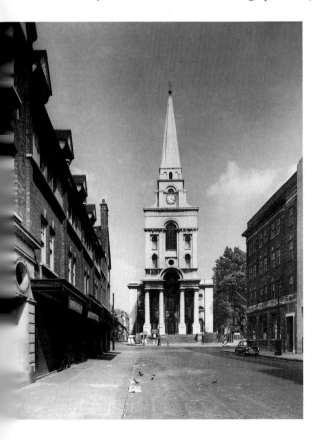

(notably the Society for the Propagation of Christian Knowledge) and charity schools, whose task was to teach poor children the rudiments of reading, writing and religion, but little more. For a while some Anglicans were also involved in the Societies for the Reformation of Manners, whose main aim was to provide information for the prosecution of whores, sabbath-breakers, drunkards, swearers and other undesirables. At their peak they brought more than three thousand prosecutions a year, but they were denounced as meddlesome killjoys and accused of caring only for the sins of the poor. Sometimes they met violent resistance: a constable was killed when trying to arrest a prostitute in Mayfair. The Societies had friends in high places, including Queen Mary, but were attacked by High Churchmen for usurping the Church's role (now moribund) in the enforcement of morality. A growing distaste for informers and for moral repression meant that by 1740 they had effectively ceased to operate.

The Church's problems after 1689 should not be seen as evidence of a collapse of religious belief. A few bold spirits challenged its very foundations, but these are interesting precisely because their arguments were new and striking. Many people scarcely came in contact with organised religion at all, especially in sparsely populated upland regions or new rootless industrial communities. But religious instincts remained strong. When Bishop Thomas Sherlock published a pastoral letter in 1750, arguing that a minor earthquake had been a punishment for London's sins, it sold over 100,000 copies. Increasingly, however, religion moved out of the political arena and became a private matter. With the Whigs triumphant in the state, Latitudinarianism prevailed in the Church. Religion became bland and anodyne: a best-selling sermon took as its text 'For His commandments are not grievous'. Increasingly religion was free of doubt, free of anguish, free of the fear of hell. Even Dissent became cooler, more introverted, with congregations less interested in winning new members than in keeping those they had. It was left to John Wesley and the Methodists to put the fire and excitement back into religion—and they were denounced as throwbacks to a more primitive age.

Under the Whig ascendancy, the Latitudinarian attitudes which had emerged under Charles II became, for the first time, widely accepted. In polite society, restraint became a mark of good breeding: enthusiasm was uncouth. At Bath and Tunbridge Wells religious disagreements were not allowed to disturb the smooth functioning of the social round. How the

---

Although the eighteenth century saw a growth of refinement and of tolerance, it was also in many ways a brutal age; violence and cruelty, especially towards animals, remained commonplace. 'The First Stage of Cruelty' by William Hogarth, 1751. The Mansell Collection

FIRST STAGE OF CRUELTY.

While various Scenes of sportive Woe
The Infant Race employ,
And tortur'd Victims bleeding shew
The Tyrant in the Boy.

Behold! a Youth of gentler Heart,
To spare the Creature's pain
O take, he cries—take all my Tart,
But Tears and Tart are vain.

Learn from this fair Example—You
Whom savage Sports delight,
How Cruelty disgusts the view
While Pity charms the sight.

Design'd by W. Hogarth.   Published according to Act of Parliament Feb. 1. 1751.   Price 1s.

lower orders felt is less certain. Wesley's mission was first and foremost to the poor, who often responded with what their betters saw as unbecoming enthusiasm. Sometimes the elite showed that it was out of touch with ordinary people. In 1736 Parliament repealed the laws making witchcraft a capital offence. Few educated people believed in witches, but many of the uneducated did and suspected witches continued to be harassed and lynched. The Jew Bill provoked an outcry which the legislators who passed it had not remotely expected. Most spectacularly of all, the Catholic Relief Act of 1780 led to the Gordon Riots in which, over several days, houses were gutted, prisons were broken open and nearly three hundred people were killed by the military.

The strength of anti-Popery in 1780 admits of no easy explanation: it was perhaps best explained by Defoe:

> 'Tis the universal scarecrow, the hobgoblin, the spectre with which the nurses fright the children and entertain the old women . . . by which means such horror possesses the minds of the common people about it that I believe there are a hundred thousand stout fellows, who would spend the last drop of their blood against Popery that do not know whether it be a man or a horse.

The force of such emotions, by no means the exclusive property of the common people, should warn us against treating the century after the Revolution as an 'age of reason', when the fanaticism of past ages was finally laid to rest. The veneer of politeness and restraint could crack to reveal more primitive, violent emotions. When the Georges refused to touch for the 'king's evil', those afflicted with scrofula touched the corpses of dead felons instead. Violence and cruelty, towards people and still more towards animals, persisted at every level of society. Even so, there are growing signs of compassion, humaneness and tolerance in eighteenth-century England. Foreigners were struck that felons were not flayed alive or broken on the wheel and that there was no religious persecution. Religious freedom, indeed, came (with some reason) to be seen as one of the great achievements of 1688. It seems most unlikely, however, that, without James II's offer of liberty of conscience, the established Church would have agreed to a toleration act. Whether, if the Revolution had not happened, James would have succeeded in establishing toleration it is impossible to say.

CHAPTER NINE

SCOTLAND

Hitherto we have dealt only with England, the biggest and richest of the three kingdoms which English kings ruled, but the impact of the Revolution was felt in Scotland and Ireland as well. As these two countries were very different from England and from each other, the Revolution affected them in different ways. Both were directly affected by what happened in England, as William and his successors used English resources in an effort to influence developments in Scotland and Ireland—more sucessfully in the latter than in the former.

In Scotland the Revolution marked an important stage in the gradual extension of England's cultural and political influence. The two kingdoms had had the same king since James VI of Scotland had become James I of England in 1603 and their Parliaments were united in 1707, but England never conquered Scotland, which remained (and remains) in many ways different from England. The slow extension of English influence north of the border could perhaps be seen as conquest by other, subtler means—a form of 'informal empire'—but two points should be borne in mind. First, English kings and ministers were rarely interested in Scotland, except as a source of potential trouble that needed to be kept quiet. It was not to be allowed to serve as a base for foreign powers, nor should disorders be allowed to develop which might have repercussions in England. In short, the English government's interest in Scotland was negative: they had no desire to exercise a positive influence on Scotland's affairs. Second, the attitude of the Scottish elite to England was ambivalent. On one hand, England was the old enemy, which flaunted its wealth and power and showed little but contempt for the Scots. On the other, that same wealth and power served as a magnet to ambitious Scotsmen. From 1603 Scotland was governed from London. Some sought favours at court, but others, like the architect Robert Adam, found Scotland 'but a narrow place' and sought 'a more extensive and more honourable scene' in which to use their talents. Moreover, however much they might resent it, many Scots recognised that England was more advanced, prosperous and civilised, a model to be copied: 'If countries have their ages with regard to improvement, North Britain may be considered as in a state of early youth, guided and supported by the strength of her kindred country.' An Irishman, Thomas Sheridan, lectured the burghers of Edinburgh on the correct pronunciation of English. In the words of David Hume, Scots 'are unhappy in our accent and pronunciation, speak a very corrupt dialogue of the tongue which we make use of.' Scots wished to be accepted as equals—hence the term 'North Britain'—but when they were not they found solace in Scottish pride and patriotism.

In the century before 1688 Scotland had slowly become more orderly. Traditionally the nobles had conducted their affairs with sublime contempt for the king's efforts to keep them in check. The king tried to play one off against another or to buy their support, but they were notoriously slippery and changed tack with bewildering frequency. By contrast, the nobles wielded great power over the lesser landowners and peasants. Most tenants had no security of tenure and were also subject to the landlord's law courts, for 'heritable jurisdictions' were passed on, like lands, from father to son. Nobles also played a large part in appointing ministers and schoolmasters and held a variety of local government offices: in short, few aspects of life fell outside their control.

During the seventeenth and eighteenth centuries, the dependence of peasant on landlord remained largely unchanged: Cobbett, on a visit to Scotland, was disgusted by the bovine resignation with which tenants accepted their lot. By contrast, the lesser landlords, or lairds, emancipated themselves to a considerable extent from the tutelage of the nobility, much as the gentry had done in Tudor England. The great nobles still dominated national politics, but the lairds increasingly directed local government: this was made easier when the Union transferred the magnates' attention to Westminster. The lairds came to dominate the Scottish civil service and legal profession and set the social tone of eighteenth-century Scotland.

With the emergence of the lairds, the law grew in importance. Noble power had rested mainly on a complex web of personal relationships, between noble and laird, and laird and tenant. This allowed of justice of a sort, as nobles and lairds adjudicated disputes and punished misdemeanours, but it was a personal and capricious justice. The law offered a more impersonal, impartial way of resolving disagreements. Scots law lacked English law's almost superstitious reverence for precedent. Procedures were changed to meet changing needs: a philosophical concern for justice was the keynote. For this reason, perhaps, it was codified comparatively late, but Sir James Dalrymple's *Institutes* (1681) showed that it could be presented as a concise and coherent system—and that the 'rule of law' was coming to be a reality as well as an ideal in Scotland.

The extension of law and order was part of the process whereby Lowland Scotland imposed its authority and values on the Highlands. There were no regional contrasts in England as stark as that which existed in

Scotland between what were almost two distinct civilisations. The Low-lands had long been mainly English-speaking, with a settled agriculture and an increasing respect for royal authority and the law. The Highlands were overwhelmingly Gaelic-speaking and pastoral, with seasonal migra-tions into the mountain pastures. Loyalties were personal, to the chief of the clan, or the chieftains—the heads of cadet branches of the same family. Kinship, real or fictitious, imposed obligations of obedience on the clansmen and of justice and protection on the chiefs. While better-off Lowlanders enjoyed some of the domestic comforts and observed some of the constraints on behaviour found south of the border, life in the High-lands was raw and elemental. Money was little used: rents were paid in cattle or labour. Chieftains entertained lavishly and drank prodigiously: wheelbarrows were sometimes provided to carry guests home. The government in Edinburgh was little more than an occasional irritant and rustling cattle (whether of Lowlanders or other clans) was a way of life. Moreover, whereas most Lowlanders were Protestants, Highlanders (inso-far as they had a religion) were mainly Catholics.

Lowlands and Highlands, then, contained different and mutually antag-onistic societies. Slowly, the Highlanders were brought to heel. The Edin-burgh government nibbled away at the chiefs' powers; at least some acts of brigandage were punished. Cromwell's armies showed that superior firepower could overcome the clans' guerilla tactics. Chiefs were encour-aged to come to Edinburgh and to have their sons educated at Lowland schools: if few clansmen spoke English, their chiefs now did. It was a slow process, but was already well under way in 1688.

Another major development in the century before the Revolution was the emergence of a deep rift within Scottish Protestantism. On one side were the Presbyterians, committed to a system of church government in which the church was independent of (and in some ways superior to) the State and in which power was vested in a hierarchy of elected bodies, culminating in the General Assembly of the Kirk. Outwardly democratic, this system (based on that of Geneva) allowed for the exercise of inquisitorial and draconian powers of moral discipline. In this, the clergy acted in conjunction with lay elders and in practice nobles and lairds exercised considerable influence over both the choice of the clergy and the Kirk's affairs.

Ranged against the Presbyterians were the Episcopalians. James VI, who regarded 'presbytery' as a threat to monarchy, reintroduced bishops into the Scottish church and his successors sought to retain them: bishops appointed by the Crown would be more amenable to royal direction than elected Presbyteries. The Presbyterians claimed that episcopacy was an alien imposition and had minimal support, but in some areas (notably the north-east) Episcopalians constituted a large majority and there were pockets of Episcopalians across much of the rest of the Lowlands. In the Highlands Presbyterianism had little support outside the vast estates of the Campbell Earls (later Dukes) of Argyll. Under Charles II, the Presbyterian majority had been restive, chafing under Episcopalian rule: the Revolution was to give them their chance.

James VII and II came to the throne with considerable first-hand knowledge of Scotland, but that did not prevent him from alienating the Scots as comprehensively as he alienated the English. As in England, when he found that the Episcopalians would not go along with his plans for the Catholics, he declared for a general toleration. He issued a Declaration of Indulgence, which provoked legal objections similar to those expressed in England. His concessions to the Presbyterians failed to win their support, merely emboldening them and demoralising the Episcopalians. When he fled, few regretted his departure. Nobles and lairds rushed to ingratiate themselves with William, leaving Scotland almost without government. They then followed the example of the English, asking William to call a Convention, which met in March 1689.

As among the English, William's coming triggered a frenetic jockeying for position. Scots who came over with him urged him not to rely on those involved in government in the 1680s, but in general everyone was out for himself and men changed tactics and sides with bewildering rapidity. The Convention's Claim of Right not only denounced James's misdeeds but declared him deposed and advanced sweeping new claims. James, it said, had tried to overthrow Protestantism and to alter the government 'from a legal limited monarchy to an arbitrary despotic power'. In future, it went on, no Catholic could become king or hold any office; the prerogative was not to override the law; Parliament was to meet frequently and freely and its consent was necessary for taxation; quartering troops (for example, to make people pay taxes) was illegal; and the use of torture was to be strictly limited. A few days later, William and Mary were proclaimed King and Queen of Scotland.

Many of these claims were already well established in England, but not in Scotland. There the Crown's powers had been more arbitrary and extensive, but their impact on the subject had been much reduced by the practical problems involved in enforcing obedience. The Scots Parliament was smaller and more easily manipulated than England's, thanks to a steering committee, the Lords of the Articles (which William was persuaded to abolish). The Claim of Right, then, was a successful attempt by the Scottish aristocracy to persuade a new king, ignorant of Scottish affairs, to grant them a freedom similar to that enjoyed in England. In the short term the Crown's powers were reduced and the Scottish Parliament enjoyed a new independence. However, the defiant, capricious way in which it used that independence tried the patience of the English ministers and provided one major argument for joining it to that of England.

Apart from its constitutional provisions, the Claim of Right asserted that Episcopacy was 'a great and insupportable grievance'. The Scots whom William had met in Holland had convinced him that Presbyterianism enjoyed overwhelming support among the Scottish people. He agreed that it should be re-established, but urged moderation and insisted that Episcopalians who swore allegiance to his regime should keep their benefices: but he offered no protection more tangible than words against the Presbyterians' vindictiveness. Episcopalian ministers were 'rabbled' out of their benefices and given no chance to show where their allegiance lay. Some survived, mainly in the north and north-east, where they had overwhelming support from their parishioners. In general, even though James had treated them shabbily and (like the Tories) they had at first seen William as a deliverer, what happened at the Revolution turned the Episcopalians against his regime. Even more than the Highland Catholics, they became the mainstay of Scottish Jacobitism.

The newfound truculence of the Scots Parliament soon became more than an irritant. When Anne's last child died in 1700 it was clear that she would be the last Protestant Stuart. The English Parliament decided, in 1701, that after her death the crown should pass to the House of Hanover. The Scots were understandably nettled that their ancient ruling house should be cast aside, without their being consulted: they were not a subject kingdom, they had just happened (since 1603) to share the same king and in 1689 the Scots' choice of William had been as free and voluntary as that of the English. With a mixture of pique and bravado the Scots Parliament asserted their right to choose their own ruler. They stated that this should be a Protestant (which ruled out the Pretender), but the last thing the English ministers wanted—especially in wartime—was a potentially hostile king in Scotland. They therefore set out to induce the Scots to negotiate terms for a union.

Many patriotic Scots have seen the Act of Union of 1707 as a disaster, a humiliating surrender of sovereignty, brought about by threats, chicanery and corruption—'the greatest political job of the eighteenth century'. In fact, the picture was more complex. Scots did not speak with one voice: the elite was split into warring factions and most politicians were more than willing to move to the lusher patronage fields of Westminster, if the price was right. Scots merchants, struggling in an increasingly competitive world, stood to profit substantially from free access to the large and affluent English market (not to mention the colonies). The English commissioners offered terms that were in many ways fair and reasonable: Scotland was to keep its Presbyterian established Church and its systems of law and education. This does not mean that Scots leaped to embrace the Union: far from it. A mixture of prejudice and principle, self-interest and misrepresentation led many to oppose it vehemently. (The parallel with Britain's joining the EEC springs strongly to mind.) If the Scots Parliament eventually agreed, this owed less to bribery than to an awareness that, as England wanted the Union, it had little choice. England had five times Scotland's population and much more than five times its wealth: the wisest course was for the Scots to negotiate the best terms they could.

After the Union the Scottish Parliament and Privy Council ceased to exist. Scotland was governed from London, which caused problems. English ministers knew little and cared less about Scottish affairs: the best that can be said is that such a situation did not make for intrusive government. There were some respects, mainly legal, in which the terms of the Act of Union were not observed, but these probably mattered less than an uneasy feeling that Scotland had lost its identity: it had become North Britain. This led some, notably Robert Burns, to turn their backs on the fashion for Englishness and to make ostentatious use of Scots dialect. Burns, indeed, compared Scotland's condition with that of the American

(Left) *The second Duke of Argyll, like many Scottish magnates after the Union, spent much of his time in London, where he exerted a great influence over ministerial policy towards Scotland. He was also one of the first Highland landowners to introduce a rigorously commercial system of estate management, which seriously weakened his clansmen's traditional loyalty to their chief. From the painting by Aikman.* Scottish National Portrait Gallery

(Right) *At Inveraray Castle, the Dukes of Argyll created a home in the grand English manner and built a model village, where tenants could be housed and kept in order. Engraving by T. Barber from a drawing by J.P. Neale, 1821.* The Trustees of the National Library of Scotland

colonies, who were seeking their freedom from English 'tyranny'. Together with Sir Walter Scott, he created a romantic, nostalgic sense of nationhood which passed into the mainstream of Scottish historical writing and which depicted the Union as a betrayal of all things Scots.

For the many in the eighteenth century, however, it had brought tangible advantages. Trade boomed: Defoe described Glasgow (incredible as it may seem now) as 'one of the cleanliest, most beautiful and best built cities in Great Britain'. The Whig aristocracy latched on, with profit, to Walpole's gravy-train. Increased contact with England accelerated the process of Anglicisation. Landlords seeking to match English standards of comfort needed to boost their incomes. They imitated English agricultural techniques and, where these were related to Scottish conditions, real increases in productivity followed. Over much of the Lowlands tenant farmers prospered and their position became more secure: good farmers were an asset to be cherished. The labourers' lot changed little. They remained wretchedly poor, housed in ramshackle cottages, huddled in smoky discomfort with their children and animals. Some improving land-

In stark contrast to the splendour of Inveraray, the Dukes' tenants on Islay lived (as they had always done) in wretched poverty and squalor. Engraving by Grignion So, from A Tour in Scotland *by Thos. W. Pennant, 1790.* The Trustees of the National Library of Scotland

lords built 'model villages', designed to improve the labourers' morals and character as well as their material conditions. Most labourers, however, lived the same harsh, drab lives as their forebears.

In the Highlands, change was more rapid and eventually more drastic. The second Duke of Argyll auctioned tenancies to the highest bidder, instead of allowing them to pass from father to son: suddenly, from being essentially personal, based on kinship and custom, the relationship between lord and peasant was to become purely commercial. His policy was not a success. At a time when the Jacobite threat was still very much alive, Highland magnates (especially Whigs) needed their tenants' loyalty: the third Duke therefore gave it a high priority when granting tenancies. This showed that the habits of centuries could not be changed overnight — but they were changing. After the 1715 rising, the government established a permanent military presence in the Highlands, based on forts like Fort William. It also began to use certain loyal clans to police the rest (the Black Watch). Such methods worked well, but their effectiveness was reduced by government parsimony. The Black Watch were drafted to fight in Germany so that in 1745 the Highlands were militarily unprepared for the Jacobite rising.

In 1746 Jacobite hopes ended in the carnage at Culloden. The Highlands had not been the prime source of Jacobite support, but the government decided that their capacity for defiance and lawlessness should be destroyed. The symbols of clan life—the kilt, the bagpipes—were outlawed; clansmen were forbidden to carry swords. Heritable jurisdictions, a major component of magnate power, were abolished. New bodies sought to 'civilise' the 'barbarous' Highlanders. The commissioners appointed to manage the estates forfeited after the '45 hoped to start new industries and inculcate habits of thrift, hard work and sobriety. The Scottish SPCK opened schools designed to teach the children godliness: unfortunately most teachers were English speakers and the children spoke Gaelic. Such initiatives accelerated the advance of Lowland values (especially the cash nexus); they gained ground among the chieftains and slowly percolated downwards. In the short term, this probably did little economic or cultural damage. The cattle trade boomed and the demand for kelp (ashes of seaweed, used in glass and other industries) also grew; the region was able to absorb an increased population. But then cattle and kelp prices fell; demand dwindled. The peasants became dependent upon the potato, while landlords looked to other products, notably sheep. Thousands were evicted, or starved when the potato crop failed. Many more emigrated. With the collapse of the old economy and the dispersal of the people, the old Gaelic culture (which had survived the efforts of the SSPCK) was confined to the few who hung on and was driven out to the periphery— the coasts and the isles.

Much of this—perhaps all—would almost certainly have happened anyway, without the Revolution or the Union. This has not prevented devotees of lost causes from linking the decline of the old Highland culture to the defeat of Jacobitism. But as one culture declined, another rose. For evidence that Scotland was much more than a cultural colony of England, we need to look at the towns and especially Edinburgh. There the tenements of the Old Town were crowded and insanitary—the word 'loo' comes from the cry of 'Gardez l'eau' as the chamberpots were emptied from upper windows—but they were the home of a vigorous intellectual life. Later the New Town was built, across the valley, a model of upmarket town planning that could stand comparison with any in Europe. The city's intellectual life drew its strength from the legal profession and the university. The former gave Edinburgh society its distinctive character—refined,

Charlotte Square, Edinburgh, with St George's Church. The New Town symbolised the capital's wealth, intellectual vitality and self-confidence. Engraving by W. Watkins from a drawing by T.H. Shepherd, London 1829. The Trustees of the National Library of Scotland

learned and convivial. That society was able to flourish because the restrictive power of the Kirk, long suspicious of the arts and of independent thought, gradually waned. As late as 1696 an Edinburgh student was executed for blasphemy; half a century later Hume was able, with impunity, to develop a philosophical system based on scepticism. Also in the 1740s, the first theatre was built in Edinburgh, disguised as a concert hall; in 1756 a sensationally popular play, *The Tragedy of Douglas*, was written by a minister of the Kirk.

It is doubtful whether such an ambience could have been found in England. Eighteenth-century Englishmen had many virtues—industry, ingenuity, business acumen—but a respect for learning was not one of them. The public schools taught classics but little else (except, according to their detractors, how to drink and swear); the two universities sank into a genteel intellectual torpor. There were some distinguished scholars, especially of theology, but too many dons did little but eat and drink—one

110

remarked pensively that a goose was a silly bird, too big for one but not big enough for two—and they had few undergraduates to distract them from their leisure. In Scotland, by contrast, each parish was supposed to have a school and a schoolmaster; not all did, but standards of literacy were probably higher than in England—if not as high as some have made out. Of the four ancient Scottish universities, Edinburgh and Glasgow were situated in major cities. Professors made part of their income from fees paid by students and the public for attending lectures. Academics were therefore more attuned to the 'real world' than their English counterparts and played a major role in the intellectual life of both Glasgow and Edinburgh. In the latter, the dominant subject was philosophy, thanks (in their different ways) to Hume and the lawyers. At Glasgow, always a commercial and industrial rather than a legal and administrative centre, the main emphasis was on what came to be known as economics (with Adam Smith) and science. The practical role of Scottish universities was symbolised by the collaboration of teacher (Joseph Black) and pupil (James Watt) in the development of the steam engine.

The distinctive and distinguished intellectual life of Scotland's two great cities is a striking testimony to its retaining a separate identity after the Union. After the union of crowns in 1603 it was probably inevitable that links between England and Scotland would become closer: it was not inevitable that England would absorb or annexe Scotland—and indeed it did not. Instead there was a partial union, in which Scotland lost its political and administrative separateness, while retaining its own legal, ecclesiastical and educational systems. It is possible that there could have been a federal political union, with some devolution of power from London to Edinburgh: many hoped for this at the time. That this did not happen was due to two features of the Revolution: the greater independence of the Scots Parliament from 1689 and the change in the succession which created the possibility that the union of crowns might be dissolved. These developments convinced the English ministers that it was against England's interests for Scotland to retain a Parliament of its own. How much difference the disappearance of its Parliament made to Scotland's development in the following century is an unanswerable question. All that can be said is that English influence on Scotland, and Lowland influences on the Highlands, did not begin or end in either 1688 or 1707.

CHAPTER TEN

IRELAND

In England and Scotland the defeat of James II's attempts at innovation was welcomed by the majority of the population (even if some of the consequences were not). The same could not be said of Ireland. There the accession of a Catholic king had led the Catholic majority to hope for an end to a century of expropriation and several centuries of English rule. It was not to be. England's superior military power enabled William to defeat the Jacobite challenge. The Protestant establishment then reinforced its dominance to a point where Catholics were almost completely deprived of political and even economic power.

Seventeenth-century Ireland was not, however, divided simply into English and Irish, Catholic and Protestant. The Catholic majority was predominantly Irish, but included a small elite of English extraction, known as the 'Old English'. Descendants of the original conquerors, these mostly saw themselves as culturally distinct from, and superior to, the native Irish. The Protestants were divided between the Episcopalian established Church of Ireland and the Dissenters. The former's adherents were chiefly of English descent—landowners, civil servants, lawyers, merchants and clergy; they lived mostly in Dublin and the major towns, or on country estates. The latter were largely Presbyterian Scots—small farmers and artisans, concentrated mainly in Ulster, a short sea-crossing from their brethren in south-west Scotland. The Dublin establishment viewed the Ulster Scots with suspicion: under Charles II it saw them as a more serious threat to the peace of Ireland than the Catholics. Religion and political antipathy combined with a certain snobbery to keep the two main elements of Irish Protestantism on terms that were less than cordial.

The expropriation of the Catholics was a gradual process. Some chieftains were deprived of their lands through legal chicanery, others forfeited them by rebellion. On the eve of the 1641 rebellion Catholics, mostly Old English, still held sixty per cent of the land. Most joined the rising, so their lands were confiscated under Cromwell; some regained their estates at the Restoration, but at James's accession their share of the land was only twenty per cent. Their self-proclaimed leader was a long-time associate of James's, Richard 'Roaring Dick' Talbot, Earl of Tyrconnell.

He sought to play on James's religious susceptibilities and to overcome James's engrained belief that the Irish were inferior to the English and that Ireland's interests should be subordinated to England's. Tyrconnell, a man of brazen cheek and great force of character, argued that only the Catholics were truly loyal to the monarchy: the Protestants, he said, were all 'Cromwellians', who persistently misrepresented the Catholics to the king and denied them the opportunity they craved to serve him. 'But since, sir,' he wrote, 'it is our lot only to suffer and not to rejoice with your majesty, we will ever do that as we ought.'

Tyrconnell's claim that all Protestants were disloyal was as misleading as his claim to represent all the Catholics. He had little fondness for the native Irish, the 'Os and Macs', and aimed mainly to re-establish the power of the Old English. The Gaelic leaders, for their part, viewed him with suspicion. Nonetheless, he persuaded James to put both the administration and the army into Catholic hands, so that when James's cause collapsed in England, Tyrconnell was able to make a serious bid to control the whole of Ireland, with a view to making it independent of England. As Protestants fled in droves, Tyrconnell's forces pushed into Ulster, until only Londonderry and Enniskillen defied them. Meanwhile, James arrived from France with French military advisers and a little military aid. He called a Parliament in Dublin, made up mainly of Old English. It passed a massive Act of Attainder, which declared forfeit the property of almost every Protestant of note. It seemed that Ireland was at last to throw off English rule.

It was not to be. The Irish military effort was a shambles, bedevilled by lack of supplies, pilfering, feuding and a chronic shortage of money: trading had ceased when the Protestants fled. The French described the Irish soldiers as 'vagabonds', 'mutineers' and 'wild bears'. The officers were inexperienced, the civilian administrators inept or corrupt. There was a desperate shortage of transport: while rifles sent by the French rusted at Cork and Kinsale, a regiment at the siege of Derry had only seven serviceable muskets. Even so, the Jacobite forces would probably have overrun Ulster but for the dogged resistance of the inhabitants of Derry and Enniskillen. Despite hunger, disease and the agonising slowness with which help arrived from England, they hung on. At the end of June, the French commander at the siege of Derry drove four thousand Protestants from neighbouring villages to the walls, aiming to force the citizens either to let them in (and so use up their food more quickly) or watch them starve. The citizens responded by firing on the villagers and threatening to hang their prisoners. Late in July James abandoned the siege, as hopeless; a few days later, the first supplies from England reached the town.

The ending of the siege denied James's forces victory: it did not condemn them to defeat. In the autumn William sent over a large army, much of which died of disease in the long wet winter. In June 1690 William arrived in person, with another large force. Louis XIV, his resources already overstretched, refused to send reinforcements. William's plan was simple: to seek out and defeat the Jacobites, relying on superior numbers and firepower. On 1 July the armies met at the River Boyne, near Drogheda. James had already planned his retreat and the broken terrain prevented much of his army from coming to grips with the enemy. There was still some fierce fighting, but casualties were limited and much of James's army withdrew in good order. Nevertheless, the way to Dublin was open and James's nerve again collapsed. '(I) do now resolve to shift for myself and so, gentlemen, must you,' he told the citizens of Dublin, and set off hotfoot for France. He never set foot in any of his kingdoms again.

The battle of the Boyne did not end the war. Despite further reverses the Jacobite forces were still undefeated at the end of the 1691 campaign. For William, the Irish war was an irritating distraction from the main war on the continent, so he was prepared to allow the Jacobites to capitulate on reasonably generous terms. The Treaty of Limerick guaranteed that many Jacobites who chose to remain in Ireland should have their liberty and property secured; those who wished to go abroad were to be transported at the government's expense. It also stated that 'the Roman Catholics of this kingdom shall enjoy such privileges in the exercise of their religion as are consistent with the laws of Ireland, or as they did enjoy in the reign of King Charles II.'

William was an honourable man with powerful Catholic allies: there is no reason to doubt his willingness to observe the terms of the treaty, both in letter and in spirit. The Irish Protestant Parliament thought otherwise. Badly shaken by recent events, especially the Act of Attainder, it set out to break the power of the Catholics once and for all. New penal laws excluded Catholics from public life and, in effect, from voting in Parliamentary elections. It was also made very difficult for Catholics to retain their land. Many who had been involved in the wars had their lands confiscated and it was enacted that in future Catholics must divide their estates equally between their sons: if one son turned Protestant, however, all the land was to go to him. By the late eighteenth century, the Catholics' share of the land had been reduced to less than five per cent: with their land, the gentry lost much of their power over the Catholic poor. Like Gaelic poets and harpers, the old landlords were still respected by the peasantry, but they could no longer offer a serious challenge to the Protestant ascendancy.

In addition to undermining the power of the Catholic landowners, the Irish Parliament set out to weaken that of the Catholic clergy. New legislation banished the Jesuits and other religious orders, along with the Catholic bishops, and tried to subject the ordinary priests to a system of registra-

Victorieus geregt van Koning William tegens den gewesen Koning Iacobus in Irland den 8 July 1690.

Koning William 2.de Hartog van Schomburg 3. Pasſeren op drie plaatſen door't Water tot de Middel en ſwemmende 4.dringen op't Vyands leger in 5.die ſy op de Vlugt krygen en Slaan

The Battle of the Boyne has long been seen as marking the end of Irish resistance to English rule; in fact the Irish capitulated on terms (which were not observed) over a year later. Contemporary Dutch engraving. BBC Hulton Picture Library

tion. For a while these measures seriously disrupted Catholic worship, but the will to enforce them soon faltered. The Pope appointed new bishops, the regulars returned and by 1731 there were about 1,700 priests in the country. There were mass-houses even in Dublin and other towns: at Cork the authorities went to an alleged 'friary', drank a bottle of wine with the friars and reported that there was no evidence of illegal Catholic activity. As bigotry waned, the ascendancy simply ignored Catholic religious life, regarding the 'superstition' of the peasantry as beneath contempt. Thus Irish Catholicism survived and even flourished. Catholic 'hedge-schools' produced an ample supply of aspirants for the priesthood—visitors remarked on the high level of literacy, even in Latin, among the peasantry. Hundreds of young Irishmen entered seminaries on the continent and by mid-century fears were even expressed that too many were being trained.

If the Irish peasantry had the consolation of their religion, in other ways their condition was grim. Like Scotland, but unlike England, Ireland had a very large number of small peasant farmers with minimal security of

115

One aspect of eighteenth century Ireland: The Festival of St Kevin at Glendalough, a Catholic peasant celebration, raucous and spontaneous. Engraving by Joseph Peacock. Ulster Museum

tenure, who scratched a living using primitive techniques: lacking harness, they would tie the plough to the horse's tail. Increasingly, they depended on the potato: a family of six was said to consume twenty-two stones (140kg) a week. Anything else they produced, including cattle, would be sold to pay the rent. Thus although Ireland produced provisions on a large scale, mainly for export to England, the peasants' diet was monotonous in the extreme, the monotony being enlivened only by illegally-distilled whiskey. While retaining considerable affection for the dispossessed Catholic proprietors, their relationship with their Protestant landlords was mixed. Some were absentees, or employed harsh stewards and middlemen; many exercised extensive judicial powers over their tenants, rather as the Scots nobles did. Some were shocked at the arbitrariness of their power: 'the poor people of Ireland are used worse than negroes', commented an English viceroy. But while their justice might be rough it seems to have been respected; moreover, landlords often protected their tenants against punishments for brawling or distilling, both important features of rural life: even religious festivals were an odd mixture of devotion, drunkenness and violence. English visitors were amazed

116

that Irish peasants did not retaliate when knocked down by gentlemen or their servants: indeed, they often showed great loyalty to 'the family' in the big house, showing every sign of 'good nature, resignation and content'. Swift spoke gloomily of their having lost 'the very notions of liberty'. A later writer offered another explanation: 'perhaps they had never known any different scenes: they were not perplexed with compound or comparative ideas.'

If the Catholic peasantry remained in their traditional servitude, the Presbyterians' position remained ambiguous. On one hand, the Church of Ireland elite saw them as socially inferior and politically suspect—but they were also fellow-Protestants and so potential allies against the Catholics. One spin-off from the battles of Whig and Tory in England was an Act of 1704 requiring all office-holders to take communion according to the rites of the Church of Ireland. This was intended to exclude all Dissenters from office (as in England), but was never wholly effective and was repealed in 1780. Exclusion from office encouraged ambitious Presbyterians (and Catholics) to make their way elsewhere, notably through trade, but many Presbyterians were little, if at all, better off than the Catholic peasantry. Although some immigrants still came to Ulster from Scotland, this influx was more than outweighed by emigrants to North America for whom even the prospect of seven years' virtual servitude was better than remaining in Ulster.

If times were hard for most Catholics and Presbyterians, for the 'ascendancy' the eighteenth century was a golden age. Exports of provisions and linen were buoyant; a rising population meant more competition for land and higher rents. Great landlords could build new houses in styles fashionable in England, lesser ones could live like lords—food, drink and servants were cheap. The Irish gentry were renowned for their lavish hospitality, even if English visitors often found their houses squalid and decrepit. Like London and Edinburgh, Dublin developed as a great centre of aristocratic social life, especially in 'Parliament-time'—the six months every second year when Parliament was in session. The great squares and public buildings of eighteenth-century Dublin were a testimony to the 'ascendancy's' affluence and good taste. Its members had more reason than most to toast the 'Glorious memory' of William and the Revolution—even if, as some remarked, the toasts served merely as a pretext to down several quarts of claret.

Besides reinforcing the Protestant ascendancy, the Revolution stimulated a growing restiveness at Ireland's subordination to England. The Irish had their own Parliament, chosen by a small electorate: the constituency of Knocktopher at one point had one elector. That Parliament's freedom was severely restricted by Poynings' Law (1494), which laid down that all bills put before it had to have the prior approval of the English

Engrav'd for the Universal Magazine 1749, for I. Hinton at y Kings Arms in S. Pauls Church-Yard LONDON.

Dublin Fireworks

This Perspective View, of the Illuminations and Fire Works, to be Exhibited at St Stephens Green at Dublin in Ireland on the Thanksgiving Day for the GENERAL PEACE, Concluded at Aix la Chapelle, 1748.

Dublin became the centre of government, politics and aristocratic social life; this is reflected in the fine squares built in the eighteenth century, such as St Stephen's Green. Engraving by T. Chambars from a painting by J. Tudor, Dublin 1749. By courtesy of the National Library of Ireland

privy council. Moreover the English Parliament, notably in the 1719 Declaratory Act, claimed that it could legislate for Ireland. At a time when even the Scottish Parliament was asserting its independence, its counterpart in Dublin found this tutelage irksome. If the Catholic peasants saw the 'ascendancy' as English, its members saw themselves as Irishmen, whose homes and whose future lay in Ireland. They thus resented the way in which Ireland's economy, like that of the North American colonies, was subordinated to English interests. England had no linen industry, so allowed Ireland's to develop unchecked, but the Westminster Parliament did its utmost to stifle Irish woollen manufacture.

The Irish Parliament was able to challenge this subordinate status because, after 1691, the Crown's revenues from Ireland were insufficient to cover the cost of government. Parliament had to be called to vote money, which gave it considerable bargaining power. The London government's main concern was to push through money bills with as little controversy as possible. The management of Parliament required a great deal of time, effort and patronage. The lord lieutenant was in overall charge, but much of the donkey-work was done by Irishmen, of whom

118

the most prominent in the early eighteenth century was William Connolly. The son of an innkeeper, he speculated shrewdly in estates forfeited after the Treaty of Limerick, helped to manage the lands of the Dukes of Ormond, married a rich wife and became involved in the revenue administration (which in Ireland, even more than England, attracted men of much ingenuity and little scruple). He ended his days as Speaker of the Irish Parliament and one of the richest men in Ireland and employed a fashionable Italian architect to build a huge house at Castletown, County Kildare, as a monument to his success.

As it was so difficult to manage the Irish Parliament, it was most unlikely that the London government would try to do more than keep Ireland quiet. The need for caution was underlined by the case of Wood's halfpence. A patent to make copper halfpennies was granted to William Wood, after he had paid a large sum to George I's mistress. Seen in Ireland as a mixture of meddling and jobbery, this grant led to a rumbling political

Speaker William Connolly rose from relative obscurity to become one of the richest men in Ireland and left a monument to his success in his great house at Castletown, Co. Kildare. By courtesy of the National Library of Ireland

The new Parliament House at Dublin (far grander than that at Westminster) symbolised both the greater independence of the Irish Parliament in the eighteenth century and the British government's concern to placate the Irish after the furore aroused by Wood's halfpence. From History and antiquities of the city of Dublin *by W. Harris, 1766.* By courtesy of the National Library of Ireland

row, which occasionally exploded into violent riots. Connolly, shrewd man that he was, came out against the patent. Others indulged in libertarian rhetoric. 'By the laws of God, of nature, of nations and of your own country,' wrote Jonathan Swift, 'you ought to be as free a people as your brethren in England': yet again, a new twist was given to the talk of 'English liberty' and 'Revolution principles' which the makers of the Revolution in England would not have welcomed. Eventually, in 1725, Wood's patent was rescinded and, as a sop to wounded Irish feelings, the British government had a new Parliament House built in Dublin, far grander than that at Westminster.

The following decades saw the British government treating Ireland with great circumspection, for fear of provoking similar outbursts of 'patriotism'. The trouble with the American colonies, however, raised feelings to new heights. Like Robert Burns, many of the ascendancy saw strong parallels between the colonists' cause and their own. Whereas Burns was an isolated individual, however, the Irish 'patriot' movement gathered momentum and, for the first time, crossed denominational lines, drawing in Presbyterians and Catholics. Fearful that Ireland might follow the American example, the British government in 1782 made major concessions, allowing Ireland freedom of trade and drastically weakening Poynings' Law. For the first time, the Irish Parliament was master of its own legislation, but this merely strengthened its hand in securing the redress of other grievances. The Declaratory Act of 1719 was repealed and a Catholic Relief Act was passed, but the solidarity which had brought about the changes of 1782 did not last for long. The French Revolution and the emergence of Catholic radicalism raised serious fears that the ascendancy might be overthrown. In the face of such anxieties, it was unable to prevent Ireland from suffering Scotland's fate and being joined to Britain in a union of Parliaments, in 1800. Thereafter Irish nationalism became mainly, but never exclusively, associated with the Catholic majority.

It may well seem that the narrow elite which ruled eighteenth-century Ireland wished to have the best of both worlds—to maintain its dominance over the Catholics while complaining of English 'tyranny'. What has happened in Ireland since 1790 would suggest that these two objectives were incompatible, but that was far from apparent at the time. For the ascendancy, the Revolution was an unmixed blessing, the source of all the felicity they enjoyed and an encouragement to seek greater autonomy within the framework of a continued association with Britain. To the Catholic gentry it meant the completion of a long process of dispossession, loss of status and exclusion from public life. For the Catholic peasantry it probably made little difference: their lives remained as impoverished and wretched as they had always been, but they bore their privations with, apparently, little complaint. For the Ulster Scots the Revolution did little to alter their fraught and ambivalent relationship with the Anglo-Irish establishment. By 1688 the situation in Ireland was such that there could be no peaceful co-existence, no compromise between the two elites, Protestant and Catholic, who both wanted the same land. As the Duke of Ormond had remarked back at the Restoration, to satisfy both would require another Ireland. In this struggle the Catholics were as intransigent as the Protestants, as the rebellion of 1641 and the attainder of 1689 made clear. At the Revolution, it was finally decided in favour of the Protestants, thanks to England's greater size and power. What implications this decision carried for the future had yet to be seen.

CONCLUSION

The Revolution of 1688 led to much oppression and injustice: men lost their lands, their livelihoods and their lives. Yet it was widely seen, first, as having saved Britain from 'Popery and arbitrary government' and, second, as opening the way for the creation of a freer, more tolerant and more prosperous society. As far as the first point is concerned, it is difficult to see James's plans as standing much chance of success (except in Ireland, where one should perhaps speak of Tyrconnell's plans rather than James's). However, the birth of his son removed the need for frenetic (and counter-productive) haste and it is just possible that, in time, he might have established toleration for Catholics and a stronger monarchy. On the second point, the trend towards liberty, tolerance and prosperity was not peculiar to England. The eighteenth century was the age of Enlightenment: men began to believe that progress could be achieved by the application of reason. Often, however, they argued that this could best be done by strengthening the monarchy and State; the real obstacles to progress seemed to be those groups and interests which stood between State and people—churches, nobles, corporate vested interests. The way forward, therefore, seemed to lie in the concentration of power and not, as in Britain, in its dispersal.

Britain thus seemed an oddity, retaining a medieval constitution in the world of 'enlightened absolutism'. What was even odder was that it seemed to work: Britain outstripped its neighbours in prosperity and developed into a major European and world power. Continentals racked their brains in search of the secret of this success; in the end they usually put it down to the quirks and contradictions of the British, or rather English, character. The problems of understanding it were set out in the first years of the nineteenth century by the poet, Robert Southey, writing in the guise of a Spaniard:

The English love to be at war, but do not love to pay for their amusement ... There is not a people upon the earth who have a truer love for their royal family than the English, yet they caricature them in the most open and insolent manner ... They cry out against

122

intolerance and burn down the houses of those whom they regard as heretics. They love liberty, go to war with their neighbours because they choose to become republicans and insist upon the right of enslaving the negroes. They hate the French and ape all their fashions ... And the common people ... boast as heartily of the roast beef of old England as if they were not obliged to be content themselves with bread and potatoes. Well may punch be the favourite liquor of the English—it is a truly emblematic compound of contrarieties.

Without dwelling overmuch on the supposed oddities of the English character, it is worth bearing these remarks in mind when considering the Revolution of 1688. It was not consciously planned, or justified in intellectually coherent terms. It was seen as conservative, yet led to major changes which many deeply resented. It was directed against 'arbitrary power', yet led to much higher taxation and the creation of a stronger State. It brought the first statutory toleration, which the majority probably deplored, but which facilitated the growth of tolerance. Again and again, we come across paradoxes or cases where things did not turn out as contemporaries expected or intended. Yet these paradoxes and complexities meant that 1688 could mean different things to different people. Conservatives could see it as justifying the status quo, radicals as an invitation to greater liberty and democracy. The libertarian generalities of the Bill of Rights came to mean something very different to later generations than they had at the time. Some were incorporated into the United States Constitution and its Amendments: the prohibition of 'cruel and unusual punishments' was recently invoked in an argument before the Supreme Court about the constitutionality of the death penalty. However much the Revolution was based on misunderstanding, however much it has subsequently been misunderstood, the fact remains that (particularly in the English-speaking world) it has made a major contribution to liberty.

SELECT BIBLIOGRAPHY

BECKETT, J. C., *The Making of Modern Ireland, 1603–1923*, Faber, 1966.

BECKETT, J. V., 'Land Tax or Excise: The Levying of Taxation in Seventeenth- and Eighteenth-Century England', *English Historical Review*, C, 1985.

BLACK, J. (ed), *Britain in the Age of Walpole*, Macmillan, 1984.

BORSAY, P., 'The English Urban Renaissance, c. 1680–c. 1760', *Social History*, V, 1977.

BREWER, J., *The Common People and Politics, 1750 to 1790s*, Chadwyck Healey, 1986.

BREWER, J. and STYLES, J. (eds.), *An Ungovernable People? The English and their Law in the Seventeenth and Eighteenth Centuries*, Hutchinson, 1980.

BURR, T. B., *History of Tunbridge Wells*, 1766.

CAIN, P. J. and HOPKINS, A. G., 'Gentlemanly Capitalism and English Expansion Overseas: I. The Old Colonial System', *Economic History Review*, Second Series, XXXIX, 1986.

CANNON, J., *Aristocratic Century: The Peerage of Eighteenth-Century England*, Cambridge, 1984.

CHILDS, J., *The Army, James II and the Glorious Revolution*, Manchester, 1980.

CLARK, J. C. D., *English Society 1688–1832*, Cambridge, 1985.

CLARK, J. C. D., *Revolution and Rebellion*, Cambridge, 1986.

CLARK, P. (ed.), *The Transformation of English Provincial Towns, 1600–1800*, Hutchinson, 1984.

CLAY, C., *Public Finance and Private Wealth: The Career of Sir Stephen Fox*, Oxford, 1978.

COLLEY, L., *In Defiance of Oligarchy: The Tory Party 1714–60*, Cambridge, 1982.

CRANFIELD, G. A., *The Press and Society: from Caxton to Northcliffe*, Longman, 1978.

CRESSY, D., 'Describing the Social Order of Elizabethan and Stuart England', *Literature and History*, III, 1976.

CRESSY, D., *Literacy and the Social Order*, Cambridge, 1980.

CRUICKSHANKS, E. (ed.), *Ideology and Conspiracy: Aspects of Jacobitism, 1689–1759*, John Donald, 1982.

DICKINSON, H. T., 'The Eighteenth-Century Debate on the "Glorious Revolution"', *History*, LXI, 1976.

DICKINSON, H. T., *Liberty and Property: Political Ideology in Eighteenth-Century Britain*, Methuen, 1979.

DICKSON, P. G. M., *The Financial Revolution in England, 1688–1756*, Macmillan, 1967.

EARLE, P., *The World of Defoe*, Weidenfeld, 1976.

FEILING, K., *History of the Tory Party, 1640–1714*, Oxford, 1924.

FERGUSON, W., *Scotland: 1689 to the Present*, Oliver and Boyd, 1968.

FRANKLE, R. J., 'The Formulation of the Declaration of Rights', *Historical Journal*, XVII, 1974.

GEORGE, M. D., *England in Johnson's Day*, Methuen, 1928.

GILBERT, A. D., *Religion and Society in Industrial England*, Longman, 1976.

GWYNN, R. D., *Huguenot Heritage*, Routledge, 1985.

HAYTER, T., *The Army and the Crowd in mid-Georgian England*, Macmillan, 1978.

HOLMES, G., *British Politics in the Age of Anne*, Macmillan, 1967.

HOLMES, G., *The Electorate and the National Will in the First Age of Party*, Lancaster University, 1975.

HOLMES, G., *The Trial of Dr Sacheverell*, Methuen, 1973.

HOPKINS, P. A., *Glencoe*, John Donald, 1986.

HOSFORD, D. H., *Nottingham, Nobles and the North*, Aubon, 1976.

JARRETT, D., *England in the Age of Hogarth*, Yale, 1976.

JENKINS, P., *The Making of a Ruling Class: The Glamorgan Gentry, 1640–1790*, Cambridge, 1983.

JOHNSTON, E. M., *Ireland in the Eighteenth Century*, Gill Macmillan, 1974.

JONES, J. R., *The Revolution of 1688 in England*, Weidenfeld, 1972.

KENYON, J. P., *Revolution Principles: The Politics of Party, 1689–1720*, Cambridge, 1977.

LANDAU, N., *The Justices of the Peace, 1679–1760*, University of California (Berkeley), 1984.

LETTS, M., *As the Foreigner Saw Us*, Methuen, 1935.

MACAULAY, T. B., *History of England*, ed. C. H. Firth, 6 vols., Macmillan, 1913.

MCKENDRICK, N., BREWER, J., and PLUMB, J. H., *The Birth of a Consumer Society*, Europa, 1982.

MCKENDRICK, N., (ed.), *Historical Perspectives: Studies in Honour of J. H. Plumb*, Europa, 1974.

MALCOLMSON, R. W., *Life and Labour in England, 1700–1800*, Hutchinson, 1981.

MATHIAS, P. and O'BRIEN, P., 'Taxation in Britain and France, 1715–1810', *Journal of European Economic History*, V, 1976.

MAXWELL, C., *Country and Town in Ireland under the Georges*, Harrap, 1940.

MILLER, J., *Bourbon and Stuart: Kings and Kingship in France and England in the Seventeenth Century*, George Philip, 1987.

MILLER, J., *The Glorious Revolution*, Longman, 1983.

MILLER, J., *James II: A Study in Kingship*, Wayland, 1978.

MITCHISON, R., *Lordship to Patronage: Scotland 1603–1745*, Arnold, 1983.

MOODY, T. W. and VAUGHAN, W. E., (eds.), *Eighteenth-Century Ireland: A New History of Ireland, IV*, Oxford, 1986.

OGG, D., *England in the Reigns of James II and William III*, Oxford, 1955.

PHILLIPSON, N., and MITCHISON, R., (eds.), *Scotland in the Age of Improvement*, Edinburgh, 1970.

PLUMB, J. H., *The Growth of Political Stability in England, 1675–1725*, Macmillan, 1967.

PORTER, R., *English Society in the Eighteenth Century*, Penguin, 1982.

PORTUS, G. V., *Caritas Anglicana*, Mowbray, 1912.

RILEY, P. W. J., *The Union of England and Scotland*, Manchester, 1978.

SHARPE, J. A., *Crime in Early Modern England*, Longman, 1984.

SIMMS, J. G., *Jacobite Ireland, 1685–91*, Routledge, 1969.

SMOUT, T. C., *A History of the Scottish People, 1560–1830*, Fontana, 1972.

SPECK, W. A., *Stability and Strife, 1714–60*, Arnold, 1977.

STEVENSON, J., *Popular Disturbances in England, 1700–1870*, Longman, 1979.

SYKES, N., *Church and State in England in the Eighteenth Century*, Cambridge, 1934.

THOMAS, K. V., *Religion and the Decline of Magic*, Penguin, 1974.

WILLIAMS, E. N., *The Eighteenth-Century Constitution*, Cambridge, 1960.

WILSON, C. H., *England's Apprenticeship, 1603–1763*, Longman, 1965.

INDEX

127